Praying with Confidence

Praying with Confidence

Aquinas on the Lord's Prayer

PAUL MURRAY, O.P.

continuum

Published by the Continuum International Publishing Group

The Tower Building 80 Maiden Lane
11 York Road Suite 704
London New York
SE1 7NX NY 10038

www.continuumbooks.com

First published 2010

British Library Cataloguing-in-Publication Data
A catalogue record for this book is available from the British Library.

ISBN 978-1441-14713-4

Typeset by Pindar NZ, Auckland, New Zealand
Printed and bound in Great Britain by the MPG Books Group

With gratitude
to three Dominican Brothers and Friends:
Robert Ombres, Jim Quigley
and
Philip McShane

*The Our Father contains all possible petitions; we cannot
conceive of any prayer which is not already contained in it. It
is to prayer what Christ is to humanity. It is impossible to say it
once through, giving the fullest possible attention to each word,
without a change . . . taking place in the soul.*

Simone Weil: *Waiting on God*

Contents

Foreword

As we meditate on the words of Fr Paul Murray's book, we have the privilege of listening in as one Dominican master interprets another. There is something distinctive about the Dominican approach to the spiritual life. Unlike the Carmelites, who place a great stress on the stages of development through which the spiritual seeker moves, and unlike the Jesuits, who emphasize the role that the human will plays in giving glory to God, Dominicans customarily speak of the God who is always already present to the one who prays. Accordingly, the Dominican writer Simon Tugwell famously extols 'the way of imperfection', that is to say, the path trod by the humble sinner whom God has deigned to address and lift up. Fr Murray, a quintessential Dominican, analyses the thought of his Order's greatest theologian, Thomas Aquinas, in regard to the prayer that Jesus gave the church – and therefore we are not surprised that, throughout this book, themes of gift and grace are paramount.

The title of our text – *Praying With Confidence* – is instructive. Fr Murray tells us that Aquinas, speaking to a crowded church in Naples in the early 1270's, declared, 'Of all the things required of us when we pray confidence is of great avail.' This is why, in teaching us to pray, Jesus put the invocation of God as 'Our Father' first. When we pray, Aquinas held, we approach the One who, out of sheerest love, created us from nothing and who subsequently, out of sheerest grace, saved us from our sin. Because of what God has done for us, we can call him 'Father' and address him in confident expectation of receiving even more gifts. Though we in no way merit such a status, we become, through prayer, the friends of God, capable of 'conversing with him in spiritual affection' and then returning to prayer with even greater boldness. There is a story told about an elderly nun who worked for many years in a Vatican office. Upon her retirement, a surprise party was held for her and she received many gifts for her long service. Her pithy speech was entirely Dominican in spirit: '*Non merito niente, ma accetto tutto* ('I deserve nothing; but I accept everything!').

To search out the ground for this spirituality is to move into very deep waters indeed, for it involves an exploration into the unique way that God exists. For Thomas Aquinas, God is not one being, however supreme, among many. God does not belong to any genus, even the genus of being, and hence cannot be classified alongside of other things. God is not, to use Thomas's technical jargon, *ens summum* (highest being) but *ipsum esse* (the act of to-be itself). And this means that God always comes first, for he is the source of whatever else exists, and that he has no need of what he makes. Since God doesn't need the world, or compete with it, or depend upon it in any sense, his relations to it are marked by utter generosity and not by the self-interested give-and-take so characteristic of our relations to one another. Hence when we pray, we are not informing God of something he doesn't know, and we are not trying to bend his will to our purposes. In point of fact, both such moves would be metaphysically impossible. Rather, when we pray, whatever is good and right in our prayer is God already praying through us, God giving us the very longing that he wishes to fulfill. Fr Murray quotes the wonderful Dominican theologian Herbert McCabe in this context: 'It is God who prays. Not just

God who answers prayers but God who prays in us in the first place. In prayer, we become the locus of the dialogue between the Father and the Son.'

I realize that this can seem puzzling, even off-putting, at first. Aren't we simply emptied out in this process, becoming God's playthings? But we have to remember that the God, who is not our rival, has absolutely no interest in manipulating us or using us for his benefit, and therefore whatever he gives us is utterly for our sake, no strings attached. When God prays in us, we become more fully alive, more completely ourselves. Fr Murray found a crucially important phrase in Aquinas's analysis of the Our Father, namely, the 'interpreter of desire'. What Thomas means is that the words of the Lord's Prayer don't compel God to act, but rather they properly order or interpret our desires. For example, when we pray 'hallowed by thy name,' we are not asking for some objective state of affairs to be re-arranged, for God's name is always hallowed; instead, we are praying that we might always place God as our highest good and highest joy. And when we pray 'thy kingdom come, thy will be done, on earth as it is in heaven', we are not attempting to force God's hand; rather, we are praying that, in the hierarchy of our long-ings, the thirst for God's righteousness might be paramount: 'seek ye first the Kingdom of God . . . and the rest will be given unto you.'

In a word, God doesn't need the Our Father, but *we* need it, which is precisely why God has given it to us. Thomas Aquinas took with utter seriousness the fact that 'God himself taught us this prayer'. If Jesus were one spiritual teacher among many, his prayer would be but a particularly simple and beautiful invoca-tion, but since Jesus is himself divine, his prayer *is* the giving of the very petitions that God wishes to answer. And this is precisely why, for Aquinas, 'the Lord's prayer stands preeminent' and is 'the most perfect of prayers'.

This book will prove to be an enormous help not only to those interested in studying the key texts of Aquinas on the Our Father, but also to all those who simply desire to pray or who desire, rather, that God might pray in and through them.

Fr Robert Barron
Francis Cardinal George Professor of Faith and Culture at Mundelein Seminary, Founder and Director of Word on Fire Catholic Ministries

Acknowledgments

My heartfelt thanks to those friends and fellow Dominicans who helped with this book in various ways; and in particular to Fathers Robert Ombres O.P., Wayne Sattler, Philip McShane O.P., Dr John F. Boyle, Brother Cassian Derbes O.P., and Dr Fainche Ryan. I would also like to thank Fr Miguel Itza O.P. and all the library staff at the Angelicum University in Rome (*Università di San Tommaso*) for their unfailing kindness and patience. A special word of thanks is also due to Adriano Oliva O.P. of the Leonine Commision. Since the critical text of St Thomas's Sermons on the Our Father has yet to appear, I am greatly indebted to Father Oliva for making available to me a provisional text of the work.

Translations into English. With respect to the *Summa theologiae*, of particular help has been the Blackfriars Latin/English edition published 1966–1975, and also the version published by Benzinger Bros. in 1948 (St Thomas Aquinas: *Summa Theologica*, trans. Fathers of the English Dominican Province). On occasion, these translations have been modified by the author. With regard to the translation of Aquinas's other works, when no name of a translator is given in the notes, the translation is by the author.

Introduction

*'But Aquinas now – he was a little too subtle, wasn't he? Does
anybody read Aquinas?'*

George Eliot: *Middlemarch*

St Thomas Aquinas was a master of the spiritual life. This fact
will almost certainly come as a surprise to those who are familiar
with the man and his work *merely* from hearsay. But, in recent
times, a number of important studies have cast a new light on this
'unknown Thomas'. In a work, for example, by the Dominican
Jean-Pierre Torrell (*Saint Thomas Aquinas: Spiritual Master*), the
author does not hesitate to declare: 'Thomas Aquinas's theology is clearly oriented towards contemplation and is as deeply
spiritual as it is doctrinal. One could say, I believe, that it is even
more spiritual than rigorously doctrinal.'[1] This claim, though an
unmistakable challenge to the popular image of Aquinas is, I am
sure, well-founded. But how, it needs to be asked, will the non-
academic reader, who has little or no professional knowledge of
theology or scholasticism, hope to encounter Aquinas as a spiritual Master? If today it is possible to speak of the 'spirituality'

---

[1]   Jean-Pierre Torrell, *Saint Thomas Aquinas: Spiritual Master*, trans.
R. Royal (Washington, DC: Catholic University of America Press, 2003;
first published in French, 1996) p. viii. See also Robert Barron, *Thomas
Aquinas: Spiritual Master* (New York: Crossroad, 1996).

1

of the great Doctor, is it something that in the end is available only to scholars and professional theologians?

For many centuries, St Thomas has been acknowledged, both within and outside the Church, as the Common Doctor – *Doctor Communis* – a title that speaks volumes. Nevertheless, in practice, the average reader can all too easily be put off by an initial encounter with the more insistently speculative and abstract character of his work. This point we find underscored, in a characteristically humourous way, by G. K. Chesterton in his celebrated book on Aquinas. He writes: 'A lady I know picked up a book of selections from St. Thomas, with a commentary; and began hopefully to read a section with the innocent heading "The Simplicity of God." She then laid down the book with a sigh and said, "Well, if that's His simplicity, I wonder what His complexity is like."'![2]

If, in Aquinas's work, there is a single point of entry which will allow the average reader immediate access to the profound and practical wisdom of the Dominican Master, I believe that point of entry can be found in St Thomas's many and various reflections on the Lord's Prayer. These reflections have, of course, sprung from the mind of a medieval scholar and theologian. Nevertheless, they are not notably obscure or difficult to grasp, being marked, for the most part, by a fine simplicity of expression, and by a content largely unencumbered by academic terminology. On occasion, in fact, St Thomas asks very simple, very direct questions, the kind of questions most people, at some stage, are likely to raise with regard to the Lord's Prayer. Why, for example, if God's name is already holy, do we say, 'hallowed be thy name'? And why do we pray, 'Lead us not into temptation', as if to suggest that God might, in some

---

[2]   G. K. Chesterton, *St. Thomas Aquinas* (London: Hodder and Stoughton, 1933) p. x.

way, be inclined to tempt us? And, since the prayer contains the phrase, 'Forgive us our trespasses as we forgive those who trespass against us', does this mean that those people who have not yet been able or willing to forgive their enemies, are unable with sincerity to pray the Our Father?

These questions, and others like them, may sound to some readers much too simple to engage, in a significant way, the attention of someone like St Thomas. But, in fact, the very opposite is the case. For, as theologian and master of the spiritual life, St Thomas possesses what Josef Pieper calls 'the art of approaching his subject from the point of view of the beginner; he is able to enter into the psychological situation of one encountering a subject for the first time . . . he sees the reality *just as* the beginner can see it, with all the innocence of a first encounter, and yet at the same time with all the matured powers of comprehension and penetration that the cultivated mind possesses.'[3] This observation, while it applies in a general way to Aquinas as author and teacher, applies in a most particular way, I would suggest, to the manner and content of Thomas's teaching on the Our Father. For, in his attempt to answer even the most obvious questions, we find him drawing instinctively on a wide range of learning and theological wisdom. And that learning, that wisdom, when fully manifest in the different reflections he makes on the prayer, betrays not merely the wisdom of an outstanding intellectual, but the wisdom also of a saint.

If we compare St Thomas's reflections on the Our Father with the celebrated meditations on the prayer composed by St Teresa of Avila, what is notably lacking in the work of the Dominican is that great surge of emotion so typical of the

---

[3] Josef Pieper, *Guide to Thomas Aquinas*, trans. C. Winston (Notre Dame, IN: University of Notre Dame Press, 1962) p. 59.

Carmelite.[4] Whereas she, as a writer, is vivid and descriptive, he, for the most part, is dogged and expository. With regard, however, to spiritual depth and wisdom, Aquinas on the Our Father more than holds his own, and emerges as a true Master. If there is one thing that particularly characterizes his work, it is, I would say, a profound reverence for Scripture, and a reverence also for the great theological and spiritual tradition which he has inherited. The Our Father, in spite of its manifest brevity, seems to allow the mind of Aquinas to range at ease over many different aspects of the Christian experience, a fact that underlines the truly comprehensive nature of this remarkable prayer. Therefore, Aquinas would have no difficulty whatsoever in agreeing with the following observation made by St Teresa of Avila: 'We ought to give great praise to the Lord for the sublime perfection of this evangelical prayer . . . I marvel to see that in so few words everything about contemplation and perfection is included; it seems we need to study no other book than this one.'[5]

A PRAYER OF ASKING

St Thomas was a theologian of prayer. But he was also, it hardly needs to be said, a man of prayer. The clarity of his thinking on the subject – the radiance of his wisdom – was something rooted in the grace of a sane, humble and whole-hearted dedication to the practice of prayer. Bernard Gui, one of the early biographers of Aquinas, writes: 'In Thomas the habit of prayer was extraordinarily developed . . . While saying Mass he was utterly

[4] St Teresa of Avila's meditations on the Our Father can be found in *The Way of Perfection*, Chapters 27–42, *The Collected Works of St. Teresa of Avila*, Vol 2, trans. O. Rodriguez and K. Kavanaugh (Washington, DC: Institute of Carmelite Studies, 1980) pp. 137–204.
[5] *The Way of Perfection*, Ch. 37, p. 183.

absorbed by the mystery, and his face ran with tears. At night, when our nature demands repose, he would rise, after a short sleep, and pray, lying prostrate on the ground.'[6] Thomas prayed not only, it is clear, out of deep theological conviction, with regard to the mysteries of the faith, but also out of a profound awareness of his own individual need for God's blessing. One prayer, attributed to him within the tradition, reads:

> To you, O God,
> Fountain of Mercy,
> I come, a sinner,
> that you would deign
> to wash away
> my uncleanness.
> O Sun of justice,
> give sight to a blind man . . .
> O King of Kings
> clothe one who is destitute.[7]

One quality that this short prayer shares with the Our Father is the fact that it is a prayer of asking, a prayer of petition. St Thomas, when he first turned his attention to the subject of prayer, as a young theologian, was quite willing to acknowledge that petition was one of its many aspects.[8] But, after years of reflection on the subject, and years also of experience as a man of prayer, he came to understand that petition is fundamental to

---

[6] Bernard Gui, *Vita S. Thomae Aquinatis*, 15, in *Fontes Vitae S. Thomae Aquinatis*, ed. D. Prümer (Toulouse: Ed. Privat. Bibliopolam, 1911) p. 183. See *The Life of St Thomas: Biographical Documents*, ed. K. Foster (London: Longmans, Green and Co, 1959) pp. 36–7.

[7] 'Oratio: pro peccatorum remissione,' *Piae preces, S. Thomae Aquinatis opuscula theologica*, Vol 1, Marietti edition (Rome: 1954) p. 289.

[8] St Thomas's first treatise on prayer (*Scriptum super libros sententiarum* IV, distinction 15, question 4) dates from about 1255–56.

the practice of prayer, Christian prayer simply cannot be understood without it.[9] By emphasising this point with such force and clarity, St Thomas was going against what was the commonly held view at the time. He was concerned, like no one else in his age, to highlight the importance of this manifestly simple yet profound form of Gospel prayer. Simon Tugwell writes:

> The great achievement of Thomas in his treatise on prayer [in the *Summa*] was to explain theologically both how prayer, in its traditional sense of petition, makes sense and how it is an authentic religious activity. He thereby shores up prayer, precisely in the sense in which all Christians are commanded to practice it. But at the same time he shows how unnecessary are a lot of the practical difficulties that people have claimed to find in prayer . . . It is at least partly thanks to Thomas that in the twentieth century two great English Dominicans could put up a fight for a straightforward and traditional account of prayer. Bede Jarrett protested against the complexity that had come to surround the practice of prayer, with the result that it had become almost impossible for many people, and Vincent McNabb asserted, against the modern tendency to dismiss petition as scarcely worthy of the name of prayer, that prayer without petition is almost blasphemous.[10]

[9]   Simon Tugwell remarks: 'It fell to the lot of Thomas [in the *Summa Theologiae*] to construct what is surely far and away the clearest and most coherent treatise on prayer since Origen. And he achieves much of his clarity by insisting on a very precise understanding of prayer as petition.' See *Albert and Thomas: Selected Writings* (New York: Paulist Press, 1988), p. 275. For a further reflection on prayer in the theology of St Thomas, see Tugwell, 'Prayer, Humpty Dumpty and Thomas Aquinas,' in *Language, Meaning and God: Essays in Honour of Herbert McCabe OP*, ed. Brian Davies (London: Geoffrey Chapman, 1987) pp. 24–50.
[10] *Albert and Thomas*, p. 275.

But what, one might ask, of the other forms of Christian prayer such as the prayer of thanksgiving, the prayer of praise and the prayer of wonder? These are, of course, 'great forms of prayer', according to McNabb. But they are not, in his opinion, 'so essentially a part of this life of struggle and trial as is the prayer of petition.'[11] Prayer – Christian prayer – by its very nature is born out of an acknowledgment of need, out of an honest recognition of spiritual poverty. In this context I find illuminating the following reflection by the contemporary Carmelite contemplative, Ruth Burrows. She writes:

> Isn't Christian existence itself petition? . . . It is the expression of dependency, of the awareness of our limitation and helplessness in so many areas. One doesn't need to have lived long to know this by experience . . . Petition, asking, is the practical admission that we are here to receive, to be 'done unto' and the deeper our faith the more we know that this is pure blessedness. We are here to receive all that God, divine Love, has to give. The Church's liturgical prayer is almost all an asking. Even the acts of praise reveal that we depend on divine aid to enable us to praise: God must praise God within us.[12]

That last statement, 'God must praise God', is unusually striking. But the idea behind it, and even the rather vivid way in which it is expressed, is something to which Aquinas, writing centuries earlier, had already given his assent. In his commentary on Psalm 39, he remarked: 'The reality, which is the object of our praise, is beyond my strength because it is greater than

---

[11] Vincent McNabb, *The Craft of Prayer* (London: Burns Oates and Washbourne Ltd, 1935) pp. 44–5.
[12] Ruth Burrows, *Letters on Prayer* (London: Sheed and Ward, 1999) p. 29.

all praise. Hence it is fitting to praise God by God (*unde Deum digne laudare est a Deo*).'[13] What this statement makes abundantly clear is that the prayer of praise and the prayer of need are, as Burrows suggested, intimately connected. Even in the very act of praise itself, God is interceding for us. And we are in manifest need of that intercession – a fact which underlines once again the importance of the prayer of petition. Burrows writes:

> Personally, I have difficulty with assertions that praise 'pure praise' is the highest form of prayer . . . But surely humble petition, the awareness of need and confidently exposing that need to God is praise, is adoration? Isn't it glorifying God's love? I think so . . . Our daily experience is of our needs, our anxieties and concerns here and now . . . who of us is not in close contact with someone in affliction of mind and body? These are things that press on our hearts and that we pray about. No Christian could possibly deny the validity of such prayer. Look at the gospels: 'Lord, if you want to, you can make me clean'; 'Lord, come and heal my child'; 'Lord, he whom you love is sick'. Our Lord made people see that he was there for them, there to be asked, there to help and there to heal. We get Paul and others exhorting their communities to lay their needs before God, lay bare their anxieties, cast their cares on the Lord, intercede for others . . . Petitionary prayer is our way of keeping in touch with God in our daily lives and what we are really doing is ensuring that God's help is there for us to endure with patience and love whatever befalls.[14]

Prayer is asking. The stark simplicity of this conclusion, although it clearly resonates with Gospel teaching, may well astonish

---

[13] Psalm 39, *In psalmos Davidis expositio*, Parma edition, Vol 14, p. 300.
[14] Ruth Burrows, *Letters on Prayer*, pp. 29–31.

those readers who have had the opportunity to study the great
spiritual texts of the sixteenth century. There, so much emphasis was given to the elevated states and stages of prayer that the
Our Father – a humble prayer of asking, a simple vocal prayer
– could quite easily appear, alongside its majestic and mystical
'relations', like a very poor cousin indeed. That, of course, was
never the intention of the great Carmelite contemplatives,
John of the Cross and Teresa of Avila. In fact, St Teresa, in *The
Way of Perfection*, spends no less than sixteen chapters reflecting on the Lord's Prayer,[15] and she also offers a robust defence
of vocal prayer itself. She writes: 'it may seem to anyone who
doesn't know about the matter that vocal prayer doesn't go with
contemplation; but I know that it does . . . I know there are
many people who while praying vocally . . . are raised by God
to perfect contemplation.'[16]

Teresa then goes on to speak about an elderly nun who came
to her once in great distress. This woman, Teresa writes, was
'never able to pray any way but vocally.'[17] She tried her best to
practice meditation, but it was useless: 'if she didn't recite vocal
prayer her mind wandered so much that she couldn't bear it.'
All she was able to do was to recite 'a certain number of Our
Fathers'.[18] But Teresa realized very quickly, as she listened to
what the nun had to tell her, that she was in the presence of a
great contemplative. 'I asked her how she was praying', Teresa
writes, 'and I saw that although she was tied to the Our Father
she experienced pure contemplation and that the Lord was

[15] St Teresa of Avila, *The Way of Perfection*, Chapters 27–42, *The Collected Works of St Teresa of Avila*, Vol 2, trans. O. Rodriguez and K. Kavanaugh (Washington, DC: Institute of Carmelite Studies, 1980) pp. 137–204.
[16] Ibid., p. 152.
[17] Ibid.
[18] Ibid.

raising her up and joining her with Himself in union.'[19] Teresa also noticed another thing, and it was a telling detail: the woman was 'living a very good life'. And so Teresa concludes: 'I praised the Lord and envied her for her vocal prayer'![20]

At one point in the *Summa*, St Thomas also discusses the question of vocal prayer. Although prayer can be described as 'the language of the heart' – St Thomas's own phrase – is it necessary, when an individual is praying in solitude, for the prayer to be vocal?[21] St Thomas replies that it is by no means necessary. Even though we are clearly invited by Jesus in the Gospel to *say* it, the Our Father need not necessarily be recited out loud. But there are occasions when it makes sense to pray vocally: 'not in order to tell God something He does not know, but so that the soul of the one who is praying and the souls of others might be lifted up to him.'[22] The interior mind is quickened, Thomas explains, by hearing the words of the prayer being spoken out loud. And this means that the prayer involves, in the end, not only the spirit but also the body, not only the *inner* heart but also the *external* voice. In this way, Thomas concludes, 'we may serve God with all that we have from God, that is, not only with our spirit but also with our body.'[23]

By emphasizing in this way the role of the body in prayer, St Thomas demonstrates a close affinity with the vision expressed in the celebrated early Dominican text, *The Nine Ways of Prayer*

---

[19] Ibid.

[20] Ibid. Elsewhere, in *The Way of Perfection*, p. 131, Teresa notes: 'I tell you that it is very possible that while you are reciting the Our Father or some other vocal prayer, the Lord may raise you to perfect contemplation.'

[21] ST, II II q. 83, a. 12.

[22] ST, II II q. 83, a. 12, ad 1. The human mind or spirit, Thomas notes elsewhere, needs to be 'taken by the hand' to God, taken or led, that is, by means of the sensible world. See ST, II II q. 81, a. 7.

[23] ST, II II q. 83, a. 12.

[*of St Dominic*]²⁴ Sometimes, Thomas notes, we find ourselves praying out loud, or praying vocally, because of an 'excess of feeling'.²⁵ And, on these occasions, there is an 'overflow from the soul into the body'. He quotes Ps. 15.9, *My heart has been glad, and my tongue has rejoiced.*²⁶ In another part of the *Summa*, when describing the prayer of adoration, St Thomas's words read almost like a gloss on the practice of prayer in *The Nine Ways*. He writes: '[A]doration consists chiefly in an interior reverence of God, but secondarily in certain bodily signs of humility; thus when we genuflect we signify our weakness in comparison with God, and when we prostrate ourselves we profess that we are nothing of ourselves.'²⁷

* * *

St Thomas and St Teresa, in their different reflections on the practice of prayer, never allow themselves to forget Jesus' own teaching on the subject. And, of course, central to that teaching are the two versions of the Our Father, which we find in the Gospels of Matthew and Luke. The Lucan passage reads: 'Now once he was in a certain place praying, and when he had finished one of the disciples said, *Lord, teach us to pray, just as John taught his disciples.* He said to them, *Say this when you pray*:

> Father, may your name be held holy.
> Your kingdom come.
> Give us each day our daily bread.
> And forgive us our sins
> for we ourselves forgive

---

²⁴ See 'The Nine Ways of Prayer (of St Dominic),' in *Early Dominicans: Selected Writings*, ed. S. Tugwell (New York: Paulist Press, 1982) pp. 94–103.
²⁵ ST, II II q. 83, a. 12.
²⁶ Ibid.
²⁷ ST, II II q. 84, a. 2, ad 2.

each person who is in debt to us.
And do not put us to the test. (Lk. 11.2-4)

In the Gospel of Matthew the text of the prayer forms part of Christ's Sermon on the Mount. It is significantly longer than the Lucan text and, perhaps for that reason, it was the Matthew version that the Church adopted for use in the Liturgy, and also for daily use by the faithful.

> Our Father, who art in heaven,
> hallowed be thy name.
> Thy kingdom come.
> Thy will be done on earth as it is in heaven.
> Give us this day our daily bread.
> And forgive us our debts,
> as we also forgive our debtors.
> And lead us not into temptation.
> But deliver us from evil. Amen. (Mt. 6.9-15)

AQUINAS AND THE OUR FATHER

'My intention is to offer higher things to the advanced while, at the same time, not refusing beginners the help they need.'[28]
St Thomas Aquinas

'God himself taught us this prayer.'[29] Few statements made

---

[28] This statement of Aquinas I have taken from its original source (a dedicatory note to a minor treatise entitled *Peri hermenieas*). I cite it here because the phrase might just as easily, I like to think, have been placed by St Thomas as an epigraph or introduction to his reflections on the Our Father. See *Peri hermenieas et Posteriorum analyticorum expositio*, Marietti edition (Rome: 1964) p. 3.

[29] St Thomas Aquinas, *The Lectures on St Matthew*, in *Albert and Thomas: Selected Writings*, trans. Simon Tugwell (New York: Paulist Press, 1988)

by St Thomas are more momentous for the spiritual life of believers and for the practice and understanding of Christian prayer. No wonder we find him noting, at one point in the *Summa*, that the Our Father is 'the most perfect of prayers'[30] and, in a sermon which he gave at Naples towards the end of his life, declaring: 'Among all prayers, the Lord's Prayer stands preeminent.'[31] St Thomas's profound regard for the Our Father is based, first and last, as he explains in the same sermon, on the fact that it was given to us by Christ 'our Advocate' and 'most wise Petitioner'.[32] Thomas quotes the First Letter of St John: *We have an advocate with the Father, Jesus Christ, the Just* (I Jn 2.1). And he adds: 'the security of this prayer is rendered the more apparent from the fact that He, who with the Father hears our prayer, did himself teach us how to pray.'[33]

Encouraged, we may presume, by the thought of the prayer's divine origin, St Thomas makes bold to say that 'people are not praying as they ought to if they are not asking for something contained in the Lord's Prayer.'[34] Of course, this doesn't mean

---

p. 455. This particular phrase comes from notes taken down during St Thomas's Lectures by the Parisian cleric, Léger de Besançon (hereafter L). The only other report, or *reportatio*, known to have survived, is by a Dominican called Peter of Andria (hereafter P). Tugwell, when translating a significant part of the *Lectures* (including the section on the Our Father) decided to fuse L and P together into a single text. (See *Albert and Thomas*, pp. 445–75). In the present study, all quotes from the *reportationes* are taken from P unless explicit reference is made to L in the notes.

[30] ST, II II q. 83, a. 9.

[31] St Thomas Aquinas, *Prologus*, No. 1019, *In Orationem Dominicam videlicet 'Pater Noster' expositio, Opuscula theologica*, Vol 2, *De re spirituali*, Marietti edition (Rome: 1954) p. 221. See 'Commentary on the Lord's Prayer,' in *The Three Greatest Prayers: Commentaries on the Our Father, the Hail Mary and the Apostles' Creed by St Thomas Aquinas*, trans. Laurence Shapcote (London: Burns Oates & Washbourne Ltd, 1937) p. 1.

[32] Ibid., *Prologus*, No. 1020, p. 221.

[33] Ibid. See 'Commentary on the Lord's Prayer,' p. 1.

[34] *The Lectures on St Matthew*, in *Albert and Thomas*, p. 454. Here St Thomas

that, when praying, we are constrained to repeat the words of the Our Father, and nothing else. We enjoy much more free- dom than that, as St Thomas is happy to acknowledge: 'Notice that the Lord does not say, "You shall pray this," but "You shall pray *like* this." He does not rule out the possibility of our praying in other words.'[35] That being said, St Thomas's original point holds true: 'if we are praying appropriately and correctly, then whatever words we may be using we are not saying anything other than what is laid down in the Lord's Prayer.'[36]

By any standards it is an extraordinary claim. But, in stating these things, Thomas is saying no more than what had already been stated many times, and with the same kind of enthusi- asm, by countless authors and theologians in the history of the Church.[37] What, however, is not perhaps generally known is the amount of time and attention Thomas devoted as a theologian to the Our Father and also, though to a significantly lesser extent, to two of the other most commonly repeated prayers of the Church: the Hail Mary, and the Apostles' Creed. Sadly, his work in this area has been generally overlooked or overshad- owed. For most readers and authors in the scholastic tradition, what has proved to be of more immediate and compelling interest, and what has drawn them over the centuries to read St Thomas, are the great exploratory and manifestly specula-

is repeating something originally stated by St Augustine in his *Letter to Proba*. See Augustine, *Ep.* 130.12.22 (PL 33.502).

[35] Ibid. In the *Summa* Thomas writes: 'Our Lord instituted this prayer, not that we might use no other words when we pray but rather that, in our prayers, we might have none but these things in view, no matter how we express them or think of them.' See II II q. 83, a. 14, ad 3.

[36] Ibid., p. 455. Here, once again, Thomas is echoing the thought of St Augustine. See *Ep.* 130.12.22 (PL 33.502).

[37] For a comprehensive summary of some of the most important reflec- tions on the Our Father in the history of the Church, see *Catechism of the Catholic Church* (Dublin: Veritas Press, 1994) pp. 586–610.

tive aspects of his writing. That, of course, is understandable. Nevertheless, the fact remains that, when he was at the height of his career as a theologian, the Our Father engaged St Thomas's attention in quite a remarkable way, and not only as a scholar but also as a preacher.

* * *

No separate book on the Lord's Prayer was ever composed by Aquinas. What he has left us, instead, are a number of texts and treatises on the subject that were composed or dictated at different times during his life. Of these texts, seven, I would say, are of particular interest. And it is the difference rather than the similarity between them that is most immediately striking.[38] On one occasion, for example, we find Thomas commenting on a Biblical text, on another, exploring a question in the *Summa* and, on another, actually preaching about the Our Father in a public church. But the voice we hear, on these occasions, is always recognizably the same voice. For, no matter what the immediate context happens to be, the mode of Thomas's discourse and the actual content of his thought remain, for the most part, remarkably consistent.

That said, however, there *are* differences. Two of the seven texts, for example (from the *Catena Aurea*) are not commentaries

---

[38] Here are the seven texts in question: a section in St Thomas's *Commentary on the Sentences of Peter Lombard*; a section from notes taken on Thomas's *Lectures on St Matthew's Gospel*; passages from the Fathers cited in the *Catena Aurea* (Gospels of Matthew and Luke); a 'question' on the Lord's Prayer in the *Summa theologiae* (II II q. 83, a. 9); a section in the *Compendium of Theology*; a series of Sermon-Conferences devoted exclusively to the Our Father. For a more detailed explanation of the character and status of St Thomas's 'writings' on the Lord's Prayer, and for information regarding the probable chronology of the different texts, see 'Appendix: Character and History of Aquinas's Texts on the Our Father,' pp. 101–5.

at all but simply a gathering of citations on the theme of the Lord's Prayer which have been lifted by Aquinas from the writings of the Fathers of the Church. Two others – one written early, the other late in Aquinas's career – are fairly straightforward academic texts composed in the scholastic manner: the first, a section in Thomas's *Commentary on the Sentences*, and the second, an article in question 83 of the Part 2 of the *Summa*. Different again are lectures St Thomas gave in Paris on St Matthew's Gospel. Although these lectures show all the signs of being composed by a medieval scholastic theologian, St Thomas's conscious aim throughout is to stay close to the text of Scripture. The result is that the work is somewhat less formal, and less systematic, than the corresponding pages in the *Summa*.[39] Two other texts of Aquinas remain to be considered: the *Compendium of Theology* and the Sermon-Conferences at Naples. Although, in the available Latin editions of the Sermons, and in the English translations of the same, we are given what appears to be a complete 'commentary' by Aquinas on each and every phrase of the Our Father, no actual report has survived of Thomas's sermon on the first of the seven petitions, *Hallowed be thy name*.[40]

---

[39] And there is also another difference to be noted between the two texts. Unlike the *Summa*, which is a highly polished work, the Matthew text is a mere *reportatio*, i.e. class notes taken down by students of Thomas, but never subsequently corrected or overseen by the Master. One of the students, who attended the Matthew Lectures, was the Dominican Peter of Andria. It has been suggested that, when he was editing his notes afterwards, Peter may have checked them against the manuscript of Thomas's Lenten Sermons (which, together with Brother Reginald, he had transcribed and turned into Latin). So there is a possibility that the text we have today of the Matthew Lectures may, in part, have been influenced by the text of the Sermons – a possibility which lends a decidedly curious status to these two late texts of Aquinas.

[40] It should be noted here that a short reflection on 'Hallowed be thy name', the first petition of the Lord's Prayer, which for centuries had been attributed to St Thomas, and which even today we find included in editions of his sermons, belongs not to St Thomas but to a

Fortunately, however, we do have available to us, in Aquinas's other writings on the Lord's Prayer, a fairly clear picture of his thoughts regarding this first petition.

The Lenten Conferences of St Thomas were not private lectures offered in a university forum, but rather public sermons delivered at the Dominican Church in Naples, and to a largely lay congregation. That fact alone explains their non-academic character. The other text, the second part of the *Compendium of Theology*, which was concerned exclusively with the Our Father, was composed in or around the same time as the Sermons,[41] and in writing it, Thomas may well have had, once again, a lay audience in mind. That is the conclusion reached by at least one commentator, Richard Regan, who goes so far as to suggest that, in contrast to the *Summa* and the *Sentences*, which were quite clearly directed towards professional theologians and active Dominican preachers, the aim of the *Compendium* was 'to provide a manual for literate, non-academic lay Christians.'[42]

Dominican friar of the late thirteenth century called Aldobrandinus of Toscanella. See B.-G. Guyot, O.P., 'Aldobrandinus de Toscanella: Source de la première petitio de editions du commentaire de S. Thomas sur le Pater,' *Archivum Fratrum Praedicatorum*, Vol 53 (1983) pp. 175–201. Aldobrandinus was a Dominican of the Roman Province. He wrote a number of books including a commentary on the Our Father, one section of which was used after his death to fill the gap in Aquinas's work. During the years, 1287–93, Aldobrandinus was lecturing in places such as Pisa, Viterbo and Siena.

[41] See J. Perrier, Review of *A propos de la chronologie du Compendium theologiae de saint Thomas* by R. Guindon, *Bulletin thomiste*, X (1957–59) p. 78. And see also 'Appendix: Character and History of Aquinas's Texts on the Our Father,' p. 101–5.

[42] Richard J. Regan (ed.) *Compendium of Theology by Thomas Aquinas* (Oxford: Oxford University Press, 2009) p. 8. The suggestion may or may not be accurate. Regan probably came to this conclusion after reading certain comments made by H.-F. Dondaine, the principal editor of the Leonine text of *Compendium theolgiae*. Dondaine, in his Introduction, remarked that, in the entire work, Aristotle was mentioned only six times,

* * *

When confronted by the question of how best to present his teaching on the Lord's Prayer, St Thomas chose, in the *Compendium*, and in the Lectures on Matthew, and in the Lenten sermons at Naples, to examine each particular phrase of the prayer in turn, and meditate on it at some length. That, as it happens, is also the method I have chosen for this short book. However, the thoughts of Aquinas on the Lord's Prayer, and the passages from his writing that I plan to cite in these pages, will not be lifted from a single text, such as the Matthew Lectures, but taken rather from any one of the seven texts of Aquinas which might, at a given moment, appear to offer the most useful and illuminating insight. It is worth noting here, in passing, that from 1270 to 1274, the last four years of St Thomas's life, not one but four of the texts under consideration were composed: the *Lectures on the Gospel of St Matthew* (ch. 6.9–15), the *Summa theologiae* (II II q. 83, a. 9), the second part of the *Compendium of Theology*, and the Lenten Sermons at Naples. That surely is evidence enough, if evidence were needed, of the importance that Thomas Aquinas, in his most mature years as a theologian, bestowed on the Lord's Prayer.

* * *

The *Compendium of Theology* was the last text St Thomas wrote on the *Pater Noster*, and he dedicated it to his confrére and secretary, Brother Reginald. The words of the dedication reveal great personal warmth for his friend, and also an active, fatherly

and that the text, being a *summary* of St Thomas's theology, was significantly less 'heavy' than an ordinary scholastic treatise. See *Compendium theologiae (seu brevis compilatio theologiae ad fratrem Raynaldum)*, in *Sancti Thomae de Aquino opera omnia*, Vol 42 (Rome: 1979) p. 8.

interest in his spiritual life. Thomas wrote: 'And so, Reginald, dearest son, I hand over to you this instruction on Christian teaching in summary form, so that you may keep it continually before your eyes.'[43] The *Compendium*, however, was never completed. The text stops abruptly just as St Thomas was reflecting on the petition *Thy kingdom come.* And that, of course, was an enormous pity, for even in its truncated form, the work is a small masterpiece. One cannot help wondering what St Thomas, had he persisted with the task, would have gone on to write afterwards. Perhaps he would have been happy to repeat, but in a different form, things he had said earlier concerning the Our Father. And if that is indeed the case, the 'compendium' or summary of those earlier reflections (which constitutes, in large part, the proposed form and aim of the present study) might well be able, paragraph by paragraph, to suggest a tentative outline of the unfinished work, and happily compose for us – within these pages – a 'manuscript' not that different, in the end, from the one St Thomas had hoped to complete for his devoted confrére, Brother Reginald, and hand over to him in order that he might keep it continually before his eyes.

---

[43] St Thomas Aquinas, *Compendium theologiae*, 1, p. 83.

1

'Our Father'

'These words raise our hopes.'[1]

There is one brief sentence in the *Compendium of Theology* that not only reveals a core conviction of Aquinas but also alerts us to the fundamental character of his spirituality. He writes: 'The confidence a human being has in God ought to be most certain.'[2] *Confidence* – that is the word, the key word, which more than any other in Aquinas's writing gives us access to his understanding of the Our Father, and indeed to his understanding of prayer in general. On one occasion, speaking to a packed church at Naples, he declared: 'Of all the things required of us when we pray confidence is of great avail.'[3] And he went on then to remark: 'For this reason . . . Our Lord, in teaching us how to pray, sets out before us those things which engender confidence in us, such as the loving kindness of a father, implied in the words, *Our Father*.'[4]

[1] St Thomas Aquinas, *The Lectures on St Matthew*, p. 458.
[2] *Compendium theologiae*, 4, p. 195.
[3] *In Orationem Dominicam*, No. 1034, p. 223. See 'Commentary on the Lord's Prayer,' p. 5.
[4] Ibid. St Thomas says something similar in his *Lectures on St John* (Jn 16.23). Prayer, he explains, arises out of the kind of love children have for their parents: 'If your prayer comes from fear, then it is not your

21

But in what sense is it true to say that God is our Father? Thomas answers this question by drawing the attention of his listeners to the mystery of creation: 'We call him Father by reason of his having created us in a special manner, viz. to his own image and likeness, which he did not impress on other creatures here below.'[5] There follows, then, this brief, wonderful statement, so characteristic of Aquinas: 'He governs us as masters of ourselves.'[6] Because of the special manner in which we were created we have, Thomas tells us, 'mastery' over our own acts. And, what is more, by being reborn in baptism, we have begun to enjoy, to an extraordinary degree, the freedom of the children of God. He quotes Rom. 8.15: 'You have not received the spirit of bondage again in fear; but you have received the spirit of adoption of sons whereby we cry: Abba, Father.'[7]

Adopted now as sons and daughters of the one Father, we are able, Thomas tells us, to live our lives in the hope of an eternal inheritance. Hope, a truly amazing hope, is quickened within us by simply saying the words 'Our Father'. In the *Compendium of Theology*, he writes:

> Through the 'spirit of adoption' that we receive, we cry: 'Abba, Father,' as it is said in Romans 8.15. For that reason our Lord began his prayer by calling upon the Father, saying 'Father' to teach us that our prayer must be based on this hope. By uttering the name 'Father', our affection is made ready to pray with a pure disposition and to obtain what we hope for.[8]

Father you are asking, but your master or your enemy.' See *Albert and Thomas*, p. 443.

[5] Ibid., No. 1028, p. 222. See 'Commentary on the Lord's Prayer,' pp. 3–4.
[6] Ibid., 'Commentary on the Lord's Prayer,' p. 4.
[7] Ibid.
[8] *Compendium theologiae*, 4, p. 195.

Not surprisingly, the word 'Father' is also the focus of attention for several entries in St Thomas's *Catena Aurea*. And of the passages cited, the one I find the most striking is the following passage from Pseudo-Augustine:

> The first word, how gracious is it? You don't dare to raise your face to heaven, and suddenly you receive the grace of Christ. From an evil servant you are made a good son. So rely not, then, on what you can do yourself, but on the grace of Christ. For, in that, there is no arrogance, but faith. To proclaim what you have received is not pride, but devotion. Therefore, raise your eyes to the Father who begot you by Baptism and redeemed you by his Son.[9]

When reflecting, in the *Summa*, on the nature of prayer, Thomas lists a number of 'conditions requisite for prayer'. One of them is that 'there should be petition.'[10] That, for Thomas, is clearly fundamental. Nevertheless, it is not the first condition he mentions. The first imperative listed is that, in one's approach to God, there should be 'a raising up of one's mind to God.'[11] This idea or statement is so simple, and so seemingly obvious, it might very easily be overlooked. But it does, I think, merit reflection. For a start, it recalls a text St Thomas included, at one point, in the Lucan *Catena Aurea*. There we are told that, as soon as we start to pray the Lord's Prayer, we should not 'break first into petition.'[12] Instead, we are encouraged, before doing anything else, to give our attention to our Father in heaven. In

---

[9] Pseudo-Augustine (*App. Serm.* 84), cited by St Thomas in *Catena Aurea*, Lk. 11.1, in *Sancti Thomae Aquinatis opera omnia*, Parma edition, Vol 12, p. 127.
[10] ST, II II q. 83, a. 17.
[11] Ibid.
[12] *Catena Aurea*, Lk. 11.1, p. 127.

other words, to 'forget all visible and invisible creatures', and 'commence with the praise of Him who created all things.'[13]

The first of the petitions in the Lord's Prayer, *Hallowed be thy name*, is focused not on the immediate attainment of our own needs but rather on the praise of God. St Thomas, in the *Compendium of Theology*, writes: 'The petition is put first because, as Chrysostom says, the person who would offer a worthy prayer to God should ask for nothing before the Father's glory, but should make everything come after the praise of Him.'[14]

That we should aim to become as self-forgetful as possible in our love and worship of God goes without saying. But love of God and love of self are not ultimately opposed. The very act of praise itself brings with it a grace of human fulfilment, and that is something St Thomas never allows himself to forget. He has no hesitation, therefore, in openly acknowledging the hidden, self-fulfilling element in even the most pure act of praise. On one occasion, he even goes so far as to include (in the *Catena Aurea*) a passage from St Augustine in which the simple 'useful-ness' of praise is emphasized. The text reads: 'In every entreaty we have first to win the good favour of the one whom we entreat, and after that mention what it is we entreat. And this we gener-ally do in praise of the one to whom our prayer is directed, and place it in front of our prayer. And that's the reason our Lord bids us say no more than, *Our Father who art in heaven*.'[15]

---

[13] Ibid. In one of his sermons at Naples, Thomas speaks of the honour we owe to God, and the first way we honour God, he says, is by giving God praise. He quotes Ps. 49.23: *The sacrifice of praise shall honour me*. And then he adds: 'this praise should be not only on our lips, but also in our heart.' See *In Orationem Dominicam*, No. 1029, p. 222. For a further reflection by St Thomas on the relationship between the prayer of petition and other forms of prayer, see ST, II II q. 83, a. 17.

[14] *Compendium theologiae*, 8, p. 199.

[15] St Augustine (*Serm. in monte*, 2, 8), *Catena Aurea*, Mt. 6.3, in *Sancti Thomae Aquinatis opera omnia*, Parma edition, Vol 11, p. 81. The

The text then changes direction, and speaks of the utter freshness and surprise of the revelation brought to us by Christ:

> Many things [in the past] were said in praise of God. But we do not find that the people of Israel were taught to address God as 'Our Father' . . . With regard to Christ's people, however, the Apostle says, *We have received the spirit of adoption whereby we cry Abba, Father and that not of our deserving, but of grace.* This, then, we express in the prayer when we say *Father.* which name also stirs up love. For what can be dearer than sons and daughters are to a father?[16]

* * *

The word 'Father' is a small word but, by pronouncing it in prayer, and in particular by repeating the phrase 'Our Father', we are achieving 'five things', Thomas tells us in his *Lectures on St Matthew*. First of all, the words 'instruct us in our faith'; second, they 'raise our hopes'; third, 'they serve to stimulate charity'; fourth, they invite us 'to imitate God'; and fifth, they call us 'to humility'.[17] The claim being made here for two small words is astonishing, though it is a claim Thomas is well able to defend. No less astonishing, in its way, at least to the uninitiated, is the dogged, intellectual manner of Thomas's exposition, his great fondness for making distinctions. This fondness, this inclination on almost every occasion, to separate out one thing from another, betrays of course the strong scholastic impulse in Aquinas, an impulse that is still operative even when he is

'pragmatism' of Augustine's viewpoint here will not be to everyone's taste. But it has at least the merit of going completely against the false 'romanticism' of the eighteenth-century Quietists and their mistaken concept of 'pure love'.

[16] Ibid.
[17] *The Lectures on St Matthew*, pp. 456–8.

engaged in the task of preaching. But, here, Thomas is speaking to us not as a preacher but as a theologian, a Master of the Sacred Page. And the first thing to which he wants to draw our attention is that, simply by saying the word 'Father', we overcome 'three errors', which, if we were to adhere to them in practice, would be fatal for our life of prayer.[18]

The first error is the idea that God is simply not concerned about us. 'On this view,' Thomas says, 'it is a waste of time asking God for anything.'[19] The second error is the idea that since everything in the world is, from the beginning, subject to a fixed fate there is no point whatever in praying. 'The third error,' Thomas says, 'concedes too much, saying that the loving providence of God is, in some way, radically changed by our prayer.'[20] Thomas, confident in his response to these challenging questions, asserts that all three errors are, in fact, 'eliminated' by the Lord teaching us to say *Our Father who art in heaven.* In the first place, being a Father, God exercises a most attentive providence over all his children.[21] And his children, his sons and daughters, are free men and women; they are not slaves subject to the constraints of necessity.[22] And, as for prayer, although it is true that it is never able to alter providence, nevertheless 'God's providence arranges for such and such a boon to be granted to us by such and such a prayer.'[23] This statement – the full meaning of this statement – contains a paradox that the human mind finds impossible to grasp. How are we to begin to understand in what way the prayers that we offer for ourselves and for others make a difference? One of the best commentators on this key

---

[18] *The Lectures on St Matthew,* p. 456.
[19] Ibid., p. 457.
[20] Ibid.
[21] Ibid.
[22] Ibid.
[23] Ibid., p. 458. This sentence is taken from L.

question is the Dominican, Brian Davies. He writes: '[T]he fact that God exists changelessly and works in everything does not mean that my prayer cannot be a cause of something coming about by virtue of God's will . . . though nothing can cause God to will what he has not willed from eternity, God may will from eternity that things should come about in accordance with my prayers and, therefore, as answers to them.'[24] And again:

> Aquinas agrees that God gives much without being asked, but he also thinks that God wants to give us some things because we ask him to do so, so that we may be confident in going to him and so that we might recognize him as the source of all good. God, says Aquinas, 'gives us many things out of sheer generosity. The reason why he wants to give us some things in response to our petition is that it is profitable for us to acquire a certain confidence in running to him, and to recognize that he is the source of all that is good for us' (ST 2a2ae, 83, 2).[25]

Acquiring confidence in the love of God, and in the willingness of God to hear and answer our prayer – that, for Aquinas, is of supreme importance. He writes: 'Prayer is offered to God not that we might make him change his mind [literally "bend him"], but that we might excite in ourselves the confidence to ask: and this confidence is particularly aroused by the consideration of his love for us . . . and that's why we say *Our Father*.'[26]

So, these two simple words, *Our Father*, not only constitute in some way a brief defence of the Christian faith, in the judgement

---

[24] Brian Davies, *Aquinas* (London: Continuum, 2003) p. 214.
[25] Ibid., pp. 213–14.
[26] ST, II II q. 83, a. 9, ad 5.

of Aquinas, they are also a wondrous – albeit tiny – revelation of its profound wisdom and teaching.

*   *   *

But why are we instructed, in the Lord's Prayer, to say 'our' and not 'my' Father? Thomas asks this question in his 'commentary' on Matthew. And he replies: 'the Lord is teaching us not to make private prayers, but to pray generally for the whole people; this kind of prayer is more acceptable to God. In Chrysostom's words, "In God's eyes a prayer is more pleasing if comes from fraternal love rather than from need." *Pray for one another* (Jas 5.16).'[27] The same question about why we say 'our' instead of 'my' is raised once again by St Thomas in the *Compendium of Theology*. This time the answer he gives places an even greater emphasis on fraternal love in the context of Christian prayer. He writes:

> Those who recognize themselves as children of God, ought, among other things, to imitate our Lord especially in love, as Ephesians 5.1-2 says: *Imitate God as his most dear children, and walk in love.* God's love is not just for one individual, but embraces all in common; for God loves 'all things that are,' as it is said in Wisdom 11.25. Most of all he loves human beings, according to Deuteronomy 33.3: *He loved the people.* Consequently, as Cyprian puts it, 'prayer for us is public and common; and when we pray, we do not pray for one person only, but for the whole people, because we are all together one people.' Or, as Chrysostom says, 'Necessity forces us to pray for ourselves, but fraternal charity impels us to pray for

---

[27] *The Lectures on St Matthew*, p. 459.

others.' And that's why we say, 'our Father,' and not simply 'my Father'.[28]

When we are saying our prayers, our hope is in God first and last. That goes without saying. Nevertheless, the prayers which we say out of kindness for others, or which others say for us, can also form part of a providential grace. '[W]e can assist one another,' Thomas notes, 'to obtain more easily what we ask for.'[29] And, by way of evidence, he quotes a short text from Jas 5.16: *Pray for one another that you may be saved.*[30] Then he continues:

> For, as Ambrose reminds us, 'many humble people [*minimi*], when they are gathered together, and are united in spirit, become powerful, and the prayers of many cannot but be heard.' This agrees with Matthew 18.19: *If two of you on earth should agree to ask anything at all, it shall be done to them by my Father who is in heaven.* Therefore we do not put forth our prayers as individuals, but with unanimous accord we cry out, 'Our Father'.[31]

---

[28] *Compendium theologiae*, 5, pp. 195–6. See also ST, II II q. 83, a. 7, ad 1.
[29] Ibid., p. 196.
[30] Ibid.
[31] Ibid. The first Christian communities prayed the Lord's Prayer together three times a day. See *Didache* 8, 3: *Sources chrétiennes* 248, 174.

2

'Who Art in Heaven'

'[T]he words, who art in heaven, *inspire us with confidence.'* [1]

In order to demonstrate how vital for the Lord's Prayer is the tiny phrase 'who art it heaven' St Thomas explains, in the *Compendium of Theology,* that these few words draw attention to the unlimited 'heavenly' power of God, and so are able to give confidence and hope to the person who is praying. He writes:

> It usually happens that when hope is lost, the reason is to be found in the powerlessness of the one from whom help was expected. The confidence characteristic of hope is not based merely on the willingness to help professed by the one in whom hope is placed: power to help must also be present. We make clear enough the readiness of the divine will to help us when we proclaim that God is our Father. But lest there should be doubt concerning the perfection of his power, we add *who art in heaven.* [2]

To the congregation at Naples Thomas remarked, in similar

---

[1]   *In Orationem Dominicam,* No. 1038, p. 224. See 'Commentary on the Lord's Prayer,' p. 6.
[2]   *Compendium theologiae,* 6, p. 196.

vein, that God is said to be 'in heaven' in order to show precisely 'the greatness of his power,'[3] and also 'to indicate his supereminence . . . seeing that he surpasses all things even our human desire and our understanding . . . Thus it is said (Job 36.26): *Behold God is great exceeding our knowledge.*'[4] Thomas notes further that the words *Who art in heaven* 'inspire us with confidence in praying in three respects: (a) as regards the power of Him to whom we pray; (b) as bringing us into familiar intercourse with Him; (c) and as being in keeping with the nature of our petitions.'[5] Because our final happiness is not here on earth but in heaven, the words *Who art in heaven* encourage us, Thomas says, to *Seek the things that are above where Christ is* (Col. 3.1).[6] What's more, the words serve as a helpful preparation for the person who utters the prayer. Thomas writes: 'This preparation should consist in imitating heavenly things, for a son should imitate his father: hence it is said (1 Cor. 15.49): *As we have borne the image of the earthly, let us bear the image of the heavenly* – in the contemplation of heavenly things, inasmuch as a man is inclined to turn his thoughts more often towards where his father is, and where those things are that he loves.'[7]

But if God is 'in heaven' and, therefore, high above us and transcendent, how is it possible for us to enjoy with God what Thomas calls 'familiar intercourse'? By way of reply Thomas

[3] *In Orationem Dominicam*, No. 1038, p. 224.
[4] Ibid., No. 1040, p. 224.
[5] Ibid., No. 1038, p. 224. See 'Commentary on the Lord's Prayer,' p. 6.
[6] Ibid., No. 1035, p. 223. See 'Commentary on the Lord's Prayer,' p. 5.
[7] Ibid., No. 1035, p. 223. See 'Commentary on the Lord's Prayer,' p. 5. In another place Thomas writes: 'The reason for saying, *who art in the heavens,* is that the heavens are the highest part of creation . . . This makes provision for the weak who are unable to rise above bodily things.' See *Lectures on St Matthew*, p. 459. The phrase 'This makes provision for the weak' comes from L.

states that God is not confined within corporeal space. He quotes Jer. 23.24: *I fill heaven and earth.*[8] God, therefore, we can say, is intimately close to us, as immanent as he is transcendent. And, what is more, He is especially close to those who, in living faith, seek to draw near to him. In the *Compendium*, St Thomas writes:

> Although God is said to be close to all human beings because of his special care for them, he is most especially close to the good who strive to draw near to Him in faith and love . . . Indeed He, not only draws near to them, he also dwells within them by grace, as Jeremiah 14.9 says: *You, O Lord, are in our midst.* Therefore, to increase the hope of the saints, we are prompted to say: 'who art in heaven' – that is, [who art] in the saints, as Augustine explains. 'For,' as he says, 'there seems to be, spiritually, as much distance between the just and sinners as there is, materially, between heaven and earth. And to signify this, we turn towards the east when we pray, because it is in that direction that heaven rises. The hope of the saints, and their confidence in prayer, are increased not only by the divine nearness, but also by the dignity they have received from God who, through Christ, has made them, in themselves, to be heavens.[9]

This means that when we speak of God being 'in the heavens', the statement can be taken, in an extended sense, to refer to God's presence in the saints on earth, those who live a heavenly life, in whom God dwells by faith.[10] Thomas repeats this idea in his St Matthew lectures: 'The heavens can be taken to mean

[8]   *In Orationem Dominicam*, No. 1038, p. 224.
[9]   *Compendium theologiae*, 6, p. 197.
[10] *In Orationem Dominicam*, No. 1036, p. 223.

the saints, as in Isaiah 1.2: *Hear you heavens,* and in Psalm 21.4: *You dwell in your holy one.* And [God] says this to give us greater confidence in obtaining what we pray for, because he is not far from us. *You are in us, Lord* (Jer. 14.9).'[11]

* * *

In the *Compendium of Theology,* when reflecting on the phrase 'who art in heaven', Thomas refers to two major obstacles which can 'stand in the way of our prayer.'[12] These obstacles, in fact, are the 'errors' of which he had already spoken briefly in the Matthew Lectures: namely, the idea, first of all, that God is simply not concerned about us; and, second, the idea that everything is subject to a fixed fate so there is no point in praying. With regard to the latter, Thomas writes:

> Some people act as though human affairs were subjected to a deterministic fatalism imposed by the stars, contrary to what is commanded in Jeremiah 10.2: 'Be not afraid of the signs of Heaven, which the heathens fear.' If this error had its way, it would rob us of the fruit of prayer. For, if our lives were subjected to a necessity decreed by the stars, nothing in our course could be changed. In vain we should plead in our prayer for the granting of some good or for deliverance from evil. To prevent this error from undermining confidence in prayer, we say: 'Who art in heaven,' thus acknowledging that God moves and regulates the heavens.[13]

---

[11] *The Lectures on St Matthew,* p. 459. The word 'far' (*longe*) does not appear in the *reportatio* of Peter of Andria but only in that of Léger of Besançon. See *Albert and Thomas,* p. 459, note 91.

[12] *Compendium theologiae,* 6, p. 196.

[13] Ibid. The translation here is by Cyril Vollert SJ. See *Aquinas's Shorter Summa* (Manchester, NH: Sophia Institute Press, 2002; first published 1947) p. 343.

At this point, Thomas goes on to speak about the other major obstacle, which, if not confronted and overcome, can have a truly deadly impact on spiritual life. He writes: 'There is another obstacle to prayer or confidence in God that would deter one from praying. This is the notion that human life is far removed from Divine Providence.'[14] In other words, the idea that God, in his divine realm, is completely indifferent to us as human beings. 'This thought,' Thomas explains, 'is given expression in the person of the wicked in Job 22.14: *The clouds are his covert. He takes no account of our affairs. He strolls around the poles of the heavens*; also in Ezekiel 9.9: *The Lord abandoned the earth; the Lord does not sees us.*'[15] 'But,' Thomas insists at once, 'the Apostle Paul demonstrated the contrary when preaching to the Athenians, saying (Acts 17.27-28): God is *not far from any of us; for in Him we live, move, and have our being.* In other words, our being is preserved, our life is governed, and our activity is directed by him.'[16]

Thomas then goes on to remark that 'not even the smallest animals are withdrawn from God's providence.'[17] He quotes Mt. 10.29-30: '*Are not two sparrows sold for a farthing? And not one of them shall fall on the ground without your Father [knowing it].*'[18] But, with regard to human beings, there is a different providence, an even greater care. Thomas writes: 'Human beings are placed under the divine care in an even more excellent way . . . our Lord says: *The very hairs on your head are all numbered*, indicating that everything belonging to us [here and now] will be recovered at the resurrection. And this ought to remove all diffidence on our part. For, as the Lord adds in the same passage: *Do not be*

[14] Ibid., 6, p. 197; Vollert, p. 344.
[15] *Compendium theologiae*, 6, p. 197.
[16] Ibid.
[17] Ibid.
[18] Ibid.

afraid, therefore, you are worth more than many sparrows.'[19] Earlier,
in the *Compendium*, St Thomas had declared: 'while Providence
watches solicitously over all creatures, it exercises special care
with regard to rational beings. For the latter are marked with
the dignity of God's image, and can attain to knowing and loving him; and, having discernment of good and evil, they have
mastery over their own actions . . . it is fitting, therefore, that
they should have confidence in God.'[20]

*   *   *

With regard to the actual form of the Lord's Prayer, St Thomas
raises an interesting question in the *Summa theologiae*. He notes,
first of all, that three of the seven petitions of the Our Father are
directed purely and simply to the glory of God: *Hallowed be Thy
name, Thy kingdom come, Thy will be done on earth as it is in heaven.*
The remaining four petitions are directed to the human hope
of enjoying that glory: *Give us this day our daily bread, and forgive
us our trespasses as we forgive those who trespass against us, and lead
us not into temptation, but deliver us from evil.* St Thomas's question is this: should the order of the petitions not be reversed,
placing the last four petitions in front of the first three, thereby
giving attention to 'the removal of evil' before thinking about
higher matters such as 'the attainment of the good'?[21] The
answer which Thomas gives immediately draws attention to the
supreme importance of desire in Christian prayer. He writes:

Because prayer is 'in some way the interpreter of our desire'
before God, we can only rightly pray for what we can rightly
desire. Now, in the Lord's Prayer, not only do we ask for all

[19]   Ibid.
[20]   Ibid., 4, p. 195.
[21]   ST, II II q. 83, a. 9, obj. 2.

that we may rightly desire, we also pray for things in the order in which they should be desired. So this prayer not only teaches us to ask, it also gives shape to our whole affective life. Now, obviously, the first thing that focuses our desire is the goal, and then the things that lead to the goal. And our goal is God. And our affection is directed toward him in two ways: first, by our willing the glory of God, and second, by willing to enjoy his glory. The first of these pertains to that love by which we love God in himself, and the second pertains to that love by which we love ourselves in God.[22]

When, during one of the conferences at Naples, Thomas spoke to the people about 'the right order of prayer', he shared with them much the same insight as he had expressed in the *Summa*. But, at Naples, he spoke in a way that was a lot easier to grasp at first hearing. After describing prayer once again as 'the inter-preter of desire',[23] he went on to remark: 'Now the right order of prayer is that our desires and prayers should prefer spiritual to carnal goods, and heavenly to earthly things: *Seek first the kingdom of God and his justice, and all these things will be added to*

---

[22] ST, II II q. 83, a. 9. That last phrase is characteristic of St Thomas. Loving God before all things does not mean ceasing to desire our own fulfilment. It does not require the repression of our natural human desire for happiness in this life and in the next. God desires to share his joy with us – *that* is the amazing truth, the stupendous detail, which St Thomas never forgets. And since our greatest joy, our greatest fulfil-ment, will in the end consist in loving God above all things, it is clear that love of God and love of self are, in a very real sense, inseparable.

[23] *In Orationem Dominicam*, No. 1022, p. 221. The phrase, 'the inter-preter of desire', is repeated in St Thomas's work a number of times. For example: ST, II II q.83, a. I, ad I; *In epistolam I ad Tim*, II, lectio I. See Jean-Pierre Torrell, 'L'interprète du désir: la prière chez saint Thomas d'Aquin', *La vie spirituelle*, 158 (May 2004): 213–23. And see also Lydia Maidl, *Desiderii interpres: Genese und Grundstruktur der Gebetstheologie des Thomas von Aquin* (München: 1994).

you (Mt. 6.33). Now our Lord teaches us to observe this order in this prayer, wherein we pray first for heavenly and afterwards for earthly blessings.'[24]

Reading over these two texts on prayer, one has the impression that, for Thomas, the innermost form of the Lord's Prayer is shaped by desire, and that, when fully awakened, desire finds expression in this prayer as in no other. Thus, without the least hesitation, he makes bold to declare in one of his Matthew Lectures: 'in this prayer all that we can desire is contained.'[25] The statement sounds definitive, the last word to be spoken on the subject. Nevertheless, so rich and many-layered is the Lord's Prayer, that St Thomas, returning at a later stage to reflect on its structure, notes that there is another way, a second way, for comprehending the inner and outer form of the prayer. In the *Compendium of Theology*, he suggests that the entire structure of the Our Father can also be seen under the rubric of the virtue of hope. What are presented to us, in the first part of the prayer, are 'the things which lead us to hope in God' and, in the second part, 'the things which we ought to hope to receive from him.'[26]

Hope, for St Thomas, the virtue of hope, is clearly at the very core of the Lord's Prayer, the key, in a sense, to understanding it. At one point he writes:

Treating, therefore, of the things contained in the Lord's Prayer, we shall make clear whatever relates to the hope of

[24] *In Orationem Dominicam*, No. 1022, p. 221. In the *Summa* we read: 'Since prayer is the interpreter of desire, the order of the petitions corresponds with the order, not of execution, but of desire or intention, where the end precedes the things that are directed to the end, and attainment of good precedes removal of evil.' ST, II II q. 83, a. 9, ad 2.
[25] *The Lectures on St Matthew*, p. 460.
[26] *Compendium theologiae*, 6, p. 197.

Christians, namely in whom it is we ought to place our hope, and for what reason, and what things we ought to hope for from Him. Our hope should be in God to whom we are to pray, as Psalm 61.9 says: *Hope in Him,* namely in God, *all you people. Pour out your hearts before him.*[27]

And again: 'Our Saviour . . . introduced us to a living hope by handing over to us a form of prayer which mightily lifts up our hope to God.'[28] This hope we can say is a *living* hope because when we pray the Lord's Prayer we are praying with a strength far greater than our own. Christ Jesus, the divine 'Advocate' and 'most wise Petitioner',[29] prays with us and for us to the Father. *That* is the ultimate basis of our confidence. Writing in the *Compendium of Theology*, St Thomas declares: '[O]ur hope reaches up to God through Christ.'[30] And he goes on to quote Rom. 5.1-2: 'Being justified by faith let us have peace with God through our Lord Jesus Christ by whom we have access through faith into this grace, in which we now stand and glory in the hope of the glory of the sons [and daughters] of God.'[31]

In the *Summa theologiae* the Lord's Prayer is described, and more than once, as 'the interpreter of desire'. Now, however, in the light of all that St Thomas has said about hope in the

[27] Ibid., 3, p. 194.
[28] Ibid.
[29] St Thomas Aquinas, *Prologus*, No. 1020, *In Orationem Dominicam*, p. 221.
[30] *Compendium theologiae*, 5, p. 196.
[31] Ibid. The Dominican Herbert McCabe reminds us again and again that, at the heart of Christian prayer, 'it is God who prays. Not just God who answers prayers but God who prays in us in the first place. In prayer we become the locus of the divine dialogue between Father and Son.' See *God Matters* (London: Geoffrey Chapman, 1987) p. 221.

Compendium of Theology, it would seem clear that this tiny Gospel prayer can just as happily be described as 'the interpreter of hope'.[32]

---

[32] As it happens, the phrase 'interpreter of hope' (*spei interpretative* or *interpres spei*) is used elsewhere by St Thomas in order to describe prayer (or petition). See, for example, Ps. 32.17, *In psalmos Davidis expositio*, in *Sancti Thomase Aquinatis opera omnia*, Parma edition, Vol 14, p. 264. And see also ST, II II q. 17, a. 2, obj. 2; and II II q. 17, a. 4, ad 3.

3

'Hallowed Be Thy Name'

'Of all desirable things the first place belongs to that one which is most lovable. This is God: and therefore you seek first the glory of God by saying Hallowed be thy name.'[1]

The petition *Hallowed be thy name*, in spite of its manifest simplicity and beauty, can appear somewhat strange at first. 'We need to look at this petition,' Thomas remarks. 'It appears to be inappropriate, because God's name is always holy, so how do we ask for it to be hallowed?'[2] This question, raised here in one of the St Matthew Lectures, Thomas answers by relying on the wisdom of the Church Fathers, citing in turn Augustine, Chrysostom

[1] St Thomas Aquinas, *In Orationem Dominicam*, No. 1108, p. 235. See 'Commentary on the Lord's Prayer,' p. 28. St Thomas makes a comparable statement in his commentary on Ps. 33.5: 'The best option is to seek God himself. That's why, in the Lord's Prayer, we ask, before anything else, *Hallowed be thy name.*' See *In psalmos Davidis expositio,* Parma edition, p. 265.

[2] *The Lectures on St Matthew,* p. 461. This sentence is taken from Peter of Andria with the exception of the last phrase which is from the *reportatio* of Léger of Besançon. Thomas raises this particular question in his reflection on the Our Father in the *Summa,* and he answers as follows: 'When we say *Hallowed be thy name* we do not mean that God's name is not holy, but we ask that men treat it as a holy thing, and this pertains to the diffusion of God's glory among men.' ST, II II q. 83, a. 9, ad 1.

41

and Cyprian.[3] And these same three names reappear, along with that of Gregory of Nyssa, in the explanation that Thomas offers in the *Compendium*. He writes: 'In order that what has begun might be completed, we say in petition *Hallowed be thy name*. This does not imply that the name of God is not holy, but rather that the name might come to be regarded as holy by all people; that is, that God should become so well known that nothing else would be considered more holy, as Augustine says.'[4]

In the form of an objection, St Thomas also addresses this question in the *Summa*. Having stated, first of all, 'It is idle to ask for something to be hallowed which is always holy, and God's name is always holy,' he replies: '*Hallowed be thy name* does not imply that God's name is not holy; it is a petition that his name may be treated as holy by human beings, and this pertains to the diffusion of God's glory among us.'[5] But how, in practice, do we come to know the name of God and, therefore, the true nature of God? In the *Compendium*, St Thomas writes: 'To some extent God makes himself known to us through a certain natural knowledge, by pouring into us the light of reason, and also by giving existence to visible creatures, in which are reflected some glimmerings of his goodness and wisdom.'[6] But 'this knowledge is imperfect because [as human beings] we cannot even comprehend creatures perfectly, and also because creatures are unable to represent God perfectly since the excellence of the cause infinitely surpasses its effect.'[7] Thomas then offers a brief overview of human history with regard to our human knowledge of God and the inevitable limitation of human knowledge. He writes:

[3] Ibid., pp. 461–2.
[4] *Compendium theologiae*, 8, p. 199.
[5] ST, II II q. 83, a. 9, obj. 1 and ad 1.
[6] *Compendium theologiae*, 7, p. 198.
[7] Ibid.

As a result of the imperfection of this knowledge, it happened that humankind, wandering from the truth, erred in various ways concerning the knowledge of God to such an extent that, as the Apostle says in Romans 1.21-23, some 'became vain in their thoughts, and their foolish heart was darkened; for, professing themselves to be wise, they became fools, and they changed the glory of the incorruptible God into the likeness of the image of a corruptible man and of birds and of four-footed beasts and of creeping things'. To recall human beings from this error, God gave them a clearer knowledge of himself in the Old Law though which humankind was brought back to the worship of the one God . . . But this information about God . . . was confined within the limits of one nation, the Jewish people, as is indicated in Psalm 75.2: *In Judea God is known; His name is great in Israel.*[8]

What was needed was an even greater revelation, nothing less in fact than a communication of the knowledge that only the Son of the living God possesses. Accordingly, Thomas writes:

In order that true knowledge of God might spread throughout the whole human race, God the Father sent the only-begotten Word of His Majesty into the world that through Him the entire world might come to true knowledge of the divine name. Our Lord Himself began this work among His disciples, as He tells us in John 17.6: *I have manifested Your name to those whom You have given me out of the world.* But His intention in imparting knowledge of the Deity was not limited to the disciples. He wished this knowledge to be promulgated through them to the whole world. This is why He adds the prayer: *That the world may believe that You have sent me.* He carries on

8   Ibid., pp. 198–9; Vollert, p. 349.

His task without intermission through the Apostles and their successors; by their ministry humankind is brought to the knowledge of God, to the end that the name of God may be held in benediction and honour throughout the entire world . . . When we say in our prayer, *Hallowed be Thy name*, we ask that the work thus begun may be brought to completion.[9]

But how exactly is the holiness of God's name to be recognized in the actual world we live in? Thomas answers: 'Among the different signs which manifest the holiness of God to human beings, the most evident sign is the holiness of those men and women who are sanctified by the divine indwelling. Gregory of Nyssa says: "Beholding the spotless life of believers, who could be so bestial as not to glorify the name invoked by such a life?"'[10] Thomas then quotes Chrysostom saying that, in giving us the words *Hallowed be thy name*, our Lord was encouraging us 'to ask that God be glorified by our lives, as if to say, make us live in such a way that all may glorify you through us.'[11] And he notes further:

> God is sanctified in the minds of others through us insofar as we are sanctified by him. Hence when we say, 'hallowed be thy name,' we pray, as Cyprian remarks, that God's name may be sanctified in us. For he himself said (Lev 11.44): *Be holy because I am holy*. Accordingly, we ask that we who have been sanctified in Baptism may persevere in what we have begun to be. Thus we pray daily to be sanctified in order that we, who daily fall, may wipe our sins away by a continual process of sanctification.[12]

9   Ibid., p. 199; Vollert, pp. 349–50.
10   Ibid., p. 199.
11   Ibid.
12   Ibid.

St Thomas, in his Matthew Lectures, expressed this last point in a no less vivid manner. He remarked: 'Every day we need sanctifying in the face of our daily sins.'[13]

* * *

The Our Father, as recorded in St Matthew's Gospel, is preceded by these words of Jesus: 'When you pray do not talk a lot, as the Gentiles do, because they think they will be heard because they talk a lot' (Mt. 6.7). One obvious way to avoid what St Thomas (echoing this text from Matthew) calls 'the much-speaking of the Gentiles,'[14] is to recite a short prayer such as the Our Father. The actual brevity of the prayer, far from being accidental, is clearly one of its most fundamental characteristics. But such a strong emphasis on brevity, is it not in some way contradicted by the command Jesus gave to his disciples in the Gospel of Luke 'to pray always and not give up' (Lk. 18.1), and by the appeal St Paul makes in his letter to the Thessalonians to 'pray without ceasing' (I Thess. 5.17)? St Thomas, when he discusses this question in his commentary on the *Sentences of Peter Lombard*, notes that 'people ought not to pray the whole time', since sometimes attention has to be given to 'works of mercy'.[15] Later, however, Thomas goes on to explain that there is, in fact, a way in which prayer can be said to *endure* even when we are actively engaged in other activities. He writes:

> The starting point of prayer is desire for eternal life, and this persists in all the other works we do in due order, because all of them should be ordered toward obtaining eternal life, and so the desire for eternal life persists virtually in all

[13] *The Lectures on St Matthew*, p. 462.
[14] Ibid., p. 454.
[15] *Commentary on the Sentences* [of Peter Lombard], Bk 4, Dist. 15, q. 4, II, (C), *sed contra*, in *Albert and Thomas*, p. 377.

the good deeds we do. This is why it says in the Gloss on I Thessalonians 5.17, 'Anyone who never stops acting well never stops praying.'[16]

This means that when we are engaged in good works, actively helping people in need, and no longer able to pray in the strict sense of the word, we are still, according to St Thomas, in some real sense living within the grace of prayer – still *praying* – because, as he remarks, 'we make the prayers of the poor our own by the help we give them.'[17] That said, however, works of mercy in themselves are no substitute for actually taking time to speak to God in prayer. Desire for God, which is the inner source of prayer, and the source also of works of mercy, needs always to be kept alive and aflame by direct and personal contact with God. 'Our desire,' Thomas says, quoting Augustine, 'grows tepid because of the cares of life, and so we call our minds back to the business of praying at certain times to make sure that desire does not freeze up entirely, once it has begun to cool.'[18] Several years later, writing in the *Summa*, Thomas raises once again the same question: 'Should prayer last a long time?', and he replies: 'it should last long enough to arouse the fervor of interior desire.'[19] When, however, fervor can no longer be sustained, 'without causing weariness' (because there is obviously no sense whatever in compelling devotion, and no reason why the mind should feel forced, as it were, to speak to God), Thomas tells us that prayer, at that point, should simply be 'discontinued'.[20]

But what if, at the time of prayer, we find ourselves plagued again and again by distractions, and our minds wander off to

[16] Ibid., Bk 4, Dist. 15, q. 4, II, (C), p. 383.
[17] Ibid., Bk 4, Dist. 15, q. 4, II, (C) 2, p. 384.
[18] Ibid., Bk 4, Dist. 15, q. 4, II, (C), p. 383.
[19] ST, II II q. 83, a. 14.
[20] Ibid.

other things? On this subject, St Thomas refuses to get worked-up, or to become unnecessarily tense and over scrupulous. He writes:

> The human spirit is unable to remain aloft for long because of the weakness of nature, for human weakness weighs down the soul to the level of inferior things. And so, when at prayer, the spirit is ascending to God by contemplation, it very quickly wanders off because of some weakness.[21]

This happens not only to the sinners among us, Aquinas notes, but also to the saints. 'Even holy men sometimes suffer from a wandering of the mind when they pray.'[22]

What really distinguishes St Thomas's approach to the subject of prayer, in contrast to that of certain other spiritual authors writing on the same subject, is an encouraging honesty and straightforwardness. There is never the least hint, for example, of false or exaggerated piety. His thought goes to the very heart of the matter. And so, more even than actual performance at prayer, what matters for St Thomas is the *intention* with which an individual sets out to pray. He remarks at one point in the *Summa*: 'to wander in mind unintentionally does not deprive prayer of its fruit.'[23] And he says further: 'it is not necessary that prayer should be attentive throughout, because the force of the original intention with which one begins prayer renders the whole prayer meritorious.'[24]

[21] ST, II II q. 83, a. 13, ad 2.
[22] ST, II II q. 83, a. 13, *sed contra*.
[23] ST, II II q. 83, a. 13, ad 3.
[24] ST, II II q. 83, a. 13. Thomas is, of course, actively concerned that we should try to be as attentive as possible when we pray. Thus he does not hesitate to declare that 'deliberately to allow one's mind to wander in prayer is sinful.' He goes on at once, however, to cite the following generous and compassionate statement from St Basil: 'If you are so truly

On the general question of distractions in prayer, there is one brief quotation from St Thomas which, given the particular focus of the present study, certainly deserves to be cited at this point. The text occurs not in the *Summa*, but in one of St Thomas's Lectures on St Paul. There, with a disarming honesty, we hear Thomas Aquinas, the celebrated philosopher and theologian, the revered master of the spiritual life, exclaim: 'it is hardly possible to say a single Our Father without our minds wandering off to other things'![25]

weakened by sin that you are unable to pray attentively, strive as much as you can to curb yourself, and God will pardon you, seeing that you are unable to stand in his presence in a becoming manner, not through negligence but through frailty.' ST II II, q. 83, a. 14, ad 3.
[25] St Thomas Aquinas, *In epistolam I. ad Corinthios*, Ch. XIV, 3, in *Sancti Thomae Aquinatis expositio in omnes s. Pauli epistolas*, Parma edition, Vol 13, p. 270.

4

'Thy Kingdom Come'

'The kingdom of God may stand for Christ himself, whom we day to day wish to come, and for whose advent we pray that it may quickly be manifested to us. Just as he is our resurrection, since in him we rise again, may he be known as the kingdom of God, because we are to reign in him.'[1]

When speaking at Naples concerning the petition, *Thy kingdom come*, St Thomas gives particular attention to the question of freedom. One of the reasons, he notes, why the kingdom of God is 'desirable' is because of 'the most perfect freedom' that exists there. Here on earth, Thomas says, 'there is no freedom, however much all desire it naturally: while in heaven there is perfect freedom without any trace of bondage.'[2]

In fact, not only will all be free, but all will be kings . . . inasmuch as all shall be of one will with God, and God shall will whatever the saints will, and the saints shall will whatever God wills. Hence, in the will of God shall their will be done. And thus all will reign, since the will of all shall be done, and God

---

[1] St Cyprian (*Tr.* vii.8), cited by St Thomas in *Catena Aurea*, Mt. 6.5, p. 82.
[2] *In Orationem Dominicam*, No. 1056, p. 226.

shall be the crown of all (Isaiah 28.5): *In that day the Lord of hosts shall be a crown of glory and a diadem of splendour for the remnant of his people.*'³

There is, in this passage, an unmistakable lift, an incantatory quality that may well indicate, on the part of Thomas, a more than ordinary enthusiasm for the theme of freedom, and an enthusiasm also, a manifest longing, for the glory of the kingdom to come.

The word 'enthusiasm' is not one that we are normally inclined to associate with St Thomas. But, again and again, we discover in the writings of the saint that, when his attention is drawn to the thought of the kingdom of God, and to the amazing freedom and joy awaiting us there, his speech, his language, becomes more urgent, more expressive than normal, his words quickened by a new and unmistakable longing. Speaking about joy, in the *Compendium*, he notes that for joy to be realized in its fullness, 'the entire affection of the joyful person must be focused on the cause of the joy.'⁴ In this life, however, being 'absent from the Lord', as St Paul puts it, and walking by faith and not by sight, that grace of undistracted contemplation is only possible in fits and starts. All the more wonderful, therefore, is the thought of what it will be like finally to see God face to face: to gaze on Him without the fear of distraction, and without intermediary. Thomas writes:

> As we have shown, in the vision of the divine essence, the created spirit possesses God as present; and the vision itself sets the affections completely on fire with divine love. If any object is lovable so far as it is beautiful and good, as Dionysius

³ Ibid.
⁴ *Compendium theologiae*, 9, p. 203.

remarks in *De divinis nominibus*, surely God, who is the very essence of beauty and goodness, cannot be gazed at without love. Therefore perfect vision is followed by perfect love. Gregory observes in one of his homilies on Ezekiel: The 'fire of love which begins to burn here on earth, flares up more fiercely with love of God when He who is loved is seen.'[5]

Thomas acknowledges that, even in heaven, the created intellect will never attain to a complete comprehension of the divine nature. But though it is true that infinite knowledge is impossible for a created intellect, nevertheless St Thomas points out that 'comprehension is promised to the saints, in the sense of the word *comprehension* that implies a certain grasp.'[6]

> Thus when one man pursues another, he is said to apprehend the latter when he can grasp him with his hand. Accordingly, 'while we are in the body,' as we read in 2 Corinthians 5.6-7, 'we are absent from the Lord; for we walk by faith and not by sight.' And so we press on toward Him as toward some distant goal. But when we see Him by direct vision we shall hold Him present within ourselves. Thus in the Song of Solomon 3.4, the spouse seeks him whom her soul loves; and when at last she finds him she says: 'I held him, and I will not let him go.'[7]

Thomas then goes on to quote Mt. 25.21: *Enter into the joy of your Lord*, and also Job 22.26: *You will then abound with delights in the Almighty*. These two texts, alongside certain words of Jesus quoted from St John's Gospel, *Ask and you shall receive, that your*

---

[5]   Ibid.; Vollert, pp. 362–3.
[6]   Ibid.; Vollert, p. 361.
[7]   Ibid; Vollert, pp. 361–2.

joy may be full (Jn 16.14), inspire Thomas to say something further about the promised joy of the kingdom. He writes:

> Since God rejoices most of all in Himself, the faithful servant is said to enter into the joy of his Lord inasmuch as he enters into the joy which his Lord enjoys. And likewise the Lord, on another occasion (Luke 22.29), made a promise to His disciples, saying: *Just as my Father appointed the kingdom to me, I appoint that you eat and drink at my table in my kingdom*. This does not mean that the saints, once they have been made incorruptible, have any use for bodily foods in that final state of good. No, by the *table* is signified rather the replenishment of the joy which God has in himself and which the saints have from Him.[8]

*   *   *

'The kingdom of God has always existed, so why then do we ask for it to come?'[9] St Thomas raises this question during one of the sermon-conferences at Naples. 'God,' he notes, 'by His very essence and nature, is Lord of all . . . And so all things ought to be subject to Him.'[10] Why, then, this second petition of the Our Father? The answer Thomas gives is short and to the point: all things on earth, he explains, are 'not yet subject' to God.[11] And the reason? Because 'sometimes sin reigns in this world: and this happens when human beings are so disposed that they follow at once the lure of sin, and carry it into effect.'[12] Of course, temptations of this kind should be resisted as much as possible. Thomas, beginning with a quotation from Rom. 6.12,

---

[8]   Ibid., 9, p. 203.
[9]   *In Orationem Dominicam*, No. 1052, p. 226.
[10]   Ibid.
[11]   Ibid.
[12]   Ibid., No. 1058, p. 227.

exclaims: *Let sin not reign in your mortal body.* But let God reign
in your heart . . . and this will be when you are ready to obey
God and keep all His commandments.'[13] Then, he adds: 'When,
therefore, we ask that his kingdom may come, we pray that
God and not sin may reign in us.'[14] The effect of this particular
prayer, he notes further, is that 'we shall obtain that beatitude
of which it is said (Mt. 5.4): *Blessed are the meek.*'[15] And again: 'if
you ask that God reign in you, Christ will also reign in you who
was most meek.'[16]

The unexpected mention here by St Thomas of one the
beatitudes calls for explanation. Why, when speaking about
one of the seven petitions, should he introduce, all of a sudden,
the subject of the beatitudes? Here, as it happens, St Thomas
is following a conscious and deliberate plan, namely, to link
every single petition in the Lord's Prayer with one of the beatitudes. And that is not all. His intention is, at the same time, to
link the seven petitions with the seven gifts of the Holy Spirit.
Not everyone in the thirteenth century, it has to be said, considered it worthwhile to try to link up, in this way, the various
dimensions of the Christian experience. The Dominican Hugh
of St Cher, for example, refused to give his attention to the
subject, remarking 'We leave that for people to argue about.'[17]
Why, in contrast, did Thomas Aquinas find the subject worth
pursuing?

When we pray the Our Father, and in particular when we say
the words, *Thy kingdom come,* what we are praying for, according to St Thomas, is nothing less than beatitude or happiness
in its highest form. And when, in the Sermon on the Mount,

[13] Ibid.
[14] Ibid.
[15] Ibid., No. 1059, p. 227.
[16] Ibid.
[17] Cited by Tugwell in *Albert and Thomas*, p. 461, note 97.

Christ speaks to his disciples concerning the beatitudes, his words represent a direct response to that human longing, to humanity's deep and urgent desire for happiness. Happiness, therefore, the search for happiness, is for Aquinas the connecting link between the beatitudes and the seven petitions of the Our Father, a link which he regards as vital, and not therefore as, in any sense, arbitrary or externally imposed.

The beatitudes themselves are concerned, for the most part, with outlining the moral and spiritual path of the believing Christian. Nevertheless, the primary rubric under which that life of virtue and holiness is lived is not obligation, as some moral theologians would have us believe, but is rather a call to infinite happiness. Since we are no longer living under the Old Law, St Thomas is able with confidence to declare, in one of the Matthew Lectures, 'the point of our beatitude is God, and the point of the virtues is beatitude.'[18] Here, I think, we can begin to grasp the determination, on the part of St Thomas, to link not only the seven beatitudes with the seven petitions but also the seven gifts of the Holy Spirit. The distinctive role of the gifts is to complete and bring to perfection those Christian virtues that we have, in some measure, already acquired. They play a vital role, therefore, in helping us to attain that final happiness which St Thomas describes as the human spirit 'adhering to God in himself by knowing and loving.'[19] And what we are praying for in the Lord's Prayer – what we are desiring – is, of course, nothing less than the attainment of that union, and the attainment also of the promised happiness of heaven, the unimaginable bliss of being able finally to see the Father without the barrier of distance, and to know him, and to love him completely.

[18] *The Lectures on St Matthew*, p. 460.
[19] *Compendium theologiae*, 9, p. 202.

By far the greatest modern commentator on the theme of happiness in the theology of Aquinas is the Dominican, Servais Pinckaers. When Pinckaers comes to reflect on the Our Father, he underlines the wonderful openness of the prayer, and how Thomas connects it with what he calls 'the search for beatitude as the ultimate end of our desires and our acts.'[20] By doing this, he notes, Thomas 'widens the horizon' in *a quite extraordinary way.*[21]

> The Lord's Prayer is no longer merely the center and point of convergence of Christian prayer. Now it is connected with the desire for happiness and, in consequence, connected also with all of human life and with morality. The teaching of Jesus on prayer joins with his teaching on beatitude . . . And so the Lord's Prayer becomes a point of principal concentration of the life of the Christian under the mode of prayer, and at the same time a center of light and of radiance for the whole of Christian morality.[22]

St Thomas's guide and master in exploring the links between the different aspects of Christian experience was St Augustine of Hippo. The distinctive mark of that influence is evident not only here, in the sermons given at Naples, but also in Thomas's early commentary on the *Sentences of Peter Lombard,* and in his great analysis of prayer in the second part of the *Summa* (II II q. 83). In the *Sentences,* we find Thomas devoting an entire article to the question of the relationship between the seven petitions of the Our Father and the seven gifts of the Holy Spirit. The answer he gives in the *Sentences,* however, is different, at least

[20] Servais Pinckaers, *La Prière chrétienne* (Freiburg: Éditions Universitaires, 1989) p. 230.
[21] Ibid.
[22] Ibid., pp. 230–1.

in one particular detail, from the answer he gives, several years later, in the *Summa*. Writing in the *Summa* he follows faithfully the links suggested by Augustine between individual petitions and individual gifts. But, in the *Sentences*, these are completely reversed. And so, for example, the gift that was linked with the first petition in the *Summa*, namely the gift of fear, is linked in the *Sentences* not with the first petition (*Hallowed be thy name*) but with the last petition (*Deliver us from evil*).

Why the young author of the *Sentences* departed from the pattern originally established by Augustine is because, by the thirteenth century, when he was writing his commentary, that 'departure' had, in fact, become the norm.[23] Years later, when Thomas was giving lectures on St Matthew's Gospel in Paris, he made it clear that both of these two ways of thinking about the Christian experience were acceptable and valid. He wrote: 'The gifts of the Holy Spirit can be fitted to these petitions in different ways, either ascending or descending. Ascending, we can attach the first petition to fear, inasmuch as fear produces poverty of spirit and makes us seek God's honour, so that we say: *Hallowed be thy name*. Descending, we can say that the final gift, that of wisdom, which makes people into God's children, goes with this petition.'[24]

Trying to hold all these links and parallels in one's mind at the same time can make one's head spin. And it may well be the case than most readers will be content to ignore the subject altogether, and join ranks with Hugh of St Cher. The telling fact remains, however, that both at the beginning and at the end of his career as a theologian, St Thomas was willing to accept the basic idea of Augustine, the notion that there is indeed a vital

[23] Ibid., p. 235.
[24] *The Lectures on St Matthew*, p. 461.

link between the petitions, the beatitudes, and the gifts.[25] In
the *Summa* (following the 'ascending' method) he offers the
following comprehensive summary of the relevant links and
parallels.

> Augustine (*De Serm. Dom in Monte*, ii, 11) connects the seven
> petitions with the gifts and the beatitudes, remarking: 'If it
> is the fear of God which makes the poor in spirit blessed, let
> us ask that God's name be hallowed among us by a chaste
> fear. If it is piety which makes the meek blessed, let us ask
> that his kingdom may come, so that we will become meek
> and no longer resist him. If it is knowledge that makes those
> who mourn blessed, let us pray that his will be done, and
> thus we will mourn no more. If it is fortitude which makes
> the hungry blessed, let us pray that our daily bread may be
> given to us. If it is counsel which makes the merciful blessed,
> let us forgive other people's sins so that our own trespasses
> may be forgiven. If it is understanding which makes the pure
> in heart blessed, let us pray that we may not have a divided
> heart, seeking temporal things which cause us to be tempted.
> If it is wisdom which makes peacemakers blessed, for they
> will be called the children of God, let us pray that we may be
> delivered from evil, because by that very deliverance we shall
> become the free children of God.[26]

St Thomas no doubt had hoped, in his sermons at Naples, to
make credible and clear the links between the petitions, the
beatitudes, and the gifts. I doubt, however, if the congregation
were able to grasp, at first hearing, the full import of what he

---

[25] For an extended reflection on this question, see Pinckaers, *La Prière
Chretienne*, pp. 231–7.
[26] ST, II II q. 83, a. 9, ad. 3.

was trying to say. A formal lecture on the subject would most probably have afforded him a more satisfactory context in which to communicate his thinking.[27] That said, however, there are times in the sermons when, even at first hearing, the links Thomas makes between the petitions, the gifts, and the beatitudes, are both sharp and revelatory.

The fact that copies of the sermons at Naples have survived is undoubtedly a cause for rejoicing. But what needs always to be remembered is that what we have in our possession are not Thomas's own revised text of the sermons, but merely notes taken down by scribes – a fact which may well obscure aspects of the spoken quality of Thomas's preaching. Was St Thomas himself a gifted preacher? Or was it perhaps the case, as Simon Tugwell has suggested, that it was 'his personal fame rather than his reputation as a preacher that drew the populace to listen to him in Naples'?[28] Part of that 'fame' was, of course, St Thomas's reputation for holiness and, we can be sure, that holiness was a key factor in the incident described here by his early biographer, Bernard Gui: 'In Rome once, in Holy Week, Thomas preached on the Passion of our Lord, moving his hearers to tears; and the next day, preaching on the Resurrection, he roused them wonderfully to joy in the Lord.'[29]

---

[27] In an early work, a commentary on *The Sentences of Peter Lombard*, St Thomas explored the links between the seven petitions in the Our Father and the gifts of the Holy Spirit. See *Scriptum super libros Sententiarum*, Bk 3, Dist.34, q. I, a. 6, in *Thomae Aquinatis opera omnia*, Parma edition, Vol 7, pp. 588–90.

[28] Tugwell, *Albert and Thomas*, p. 259.

[29] Bernard Gui, *Vita S. Thomae Aquinatis*, 29, in *Fontes Vitae S. Thomae Aquinatis*, ed. D. Prümer (Toulouse: 1911) p. 195. See *The Life of St Thomas Aquinas: Biographical Documents*, ed. K. Foster (London: Longmans, Green and CO, 1959) p. 48.

5

'Thy will be done on earth as it is in heaven'

'See how excellently this follows; having taught us first to desire heavenly things by saying, Thy kingdom come, *now he bids us, before we come to heaven, to make this earth into heaven, saying,* Thy will be done on earth as it is in heaven.'[1]

The third petition, *Thy will be done on earth as it is in heaven*, is linked by St Thomas with the Spirit's gift of knowledge. He writes:

Of all the things which go towards building up in us knowledge and wisdom, the principal thing is that we do not cling to our own opinion. *Don't lean on your own prudence* (Prov 3.5). Those who cling to their own opinion, so that they do not trust others but only themselves, invariably prove themselves to be fools, and are adjudged as such. *Have you seen a man wise in his own conceit? There is more hope for a fool than for him!* (Prov 26.12). If, on the other hand, we don't cling to our own opinion, this comes from humility. *Where there is humility there*

---

[1]   St Chrysostom (*In hom. 20 super Matth*), cited by St Thomas, *Catena Aurea*, Mt. 6.6, p. 82.

is wisdom (Prov 11.2). The proud trust only themselves. The Holy Spirit, therefore, teaches us, by the gift of wisdom, not to do our own will but God's will. And, by virtue of this gift, we pray God that his will be done on earth as it is in heaven. And in this is seen the gift of wisdom.[2]

But what is God's will exactly? What does Christ mean when he commands us to say: *Thy will be done on earth as it is in heaven?* During one of the sermon-conferences at Naples, St Thomas asked this particular question, and he answered as follows: 'God wills three things in our regard, which we pray to be fulfilled': the first is 'that we may have eternal life'; the second is 'that we keep his commandments'; and the third is 'that we be restored to the state and dignity in which the first man was created.'[3] Regarding the first of these, Thomas writes:

When a thing attains the end for which it was made it is said to be saved; and when this is not accomplished it is said to be lost. Now God made us for eternal life and, consequently, when we gain eternal life, we are saved. This is what God desires: *This is the will of my Father who sent me that all those who see the Son, and believe in him, may have eternal life* (Jn 6.40). This will is already fulfilled in the angels and saints in the fatherland, for they see, and know, and enjoy God. We, however, desire that, just as the will of God is fulfilled in the blessed in heaven, even so it may be fulfilled in us who are on earth. This is the sense of our prayer: *Thy will be done* in us, who are on earth as it is in the saints in heaven.[4]

---

[2] *In Orationem Dominicam*, No. 1060, p. 227.
[3] Ibid., Nos 1063–7, pp. 227–8.
[4] Ibid., No. 1064, p. 228.

With regard to the second thing God wills for us, Thomas writes: 'When we say *Thy will be done*, we pray that we may keep God's commandments. This will of God is fulfilled in the righteous, but is not yet fulfilled in sinners. Now the righteous are signified by *heaven*, and the sinners by the *earth*. Hence we pray that God's will be done on *earth*, i.e. in sinners, even as it is done in *heaven*, i.e. in the righteous.'[5] Thomas makes much of the fact that this petition does not invite us to say to God something like *Let us do your will on earth*, as if we, by our own human efforts, could somehow attain to the righteousness of heaven. Thomas writes: 'Presume not, therefore, on your own strength, but trust in the grace of God.'[6] At the same time, the petition certainly does not invite us to leave everything to God, and ask nothing from ourselves. The petition does not say, for example, *Do your will*, 'as if our human will and zeal were of no account', but rather: *May your will be done* – that is: 'by the grace of God and with effort and solicitude on our part.'[7] The reason, Thomas says, 'is that two things are needed in order to obtain eternal life: God's grace and human will. Although God made us without us, he will not justify us without our cooperation.'[8]

The third thing that God wills with regard to us is 'that humanity be restored to its [original] pristine state, in order that flesh would no more rebel against spirit: *For this is the will of God, your sanctification* (I Thess 4.3)'.[9] The original state enjoyed by human beings was so great, Thomas says, 'the soul and spirit experienced no resistance from sensuality and the

---

[5] Ibid., No. 1065, p. 228. See 'Commentary on the Lord's Prayer', p. 15.
[6] Ibid., No. 1066, p. 228.
[7] Ibid.
[8] Ibid.
[9] Ibid., No. 1067, p. 228.

flesh'.[10] He writes: 'as long as the soul was subject to God, the flesh was in such subjection to the spirit, no corruption of death, or weakness, or any other passions were felt.'[11] Here, it is interesting to note St Thomas does not blame 'the flesh' for the loss of that wondrous, original harmony, as Christian commentators have been inclined to do over the centuries. No – the fault, in Thomas's opinion, was decidedly, and from the very beginning, with the *spirit*. Thomas writes: 'From the moment that the spirit and the soul, which were between God and the flesh, rebelled against God by sin, there and then the body rebelled against the soul. And, from that time, death and weakness began to be felt, as well as a continual rebellion of the flesh against the spirit.'[12] It is only in the lives of very good and saintly people (those whose spirit is 'righteous') that we can say God's will is being done on earth. 'Accordingly, when we say, *Thy will be done*, we are praying that his will may also be done regarding the flesh . . . Thus the sense of "Thy will be done *on earth*" is that it may be done for our flesh, and "as it is *in heaven*" means in our spirit by righteousness.'[13]

The beatitude which Thomas links with this third petition is the beatitude of mourning: *Blessed are they that mourn for they shall be comforted* (Mt. 5.5). As human beings, all of us 'desire eternal life'. But that life of blessing is one which we are not yet able to enjoy here on earth. And so, no matter how intense our desire, or how profound our longing, we still have to wait, and the delay causes us to mourn: '*Woe is me that my sojourn is prolonged* (Psalm 119.5).'[14] Thomas then goes on to note that there is another reason why we mourn here on earth, and it has to do with our

[10] Ibid.
[11] Ibid.
[12] Ibid.
[13] Ibid., No. 1068, pp. 228–9.
[14] Ibid., No. 1069, p. 229.

struggle to keep the commandments. He writes: 'however sweet the commandments may be to the soul, they are bitter to the flesh, which is continually buffeted: *Going, they went and wept*, which refers to the flesh, *But coming, they shall come with joyfulness*, which refers to the soul (Psalm 125.6).'[15] Finally, Thomas remarks, speaking with an impressive, down-to-earth realism,

> sorrow results from the continual conflict between the flesh and the spirit: since it is impossible for the soul not to be wounded at least by venial sins due to the flesh; and so in doing expiation for these, the soul is in mourning: *Every night*, that is, in the darkness of sin, *I will wash my bed*, that is, my conscience, *with tears* (Psalm 6.7). Those who weep thus will reach their heavenly country, whereto may God bring us all.[16]

* * *

The challenging truth that, 'however sweet the commandments are to the soul, they are bitter to the flesh',[17] is expressed by Thomas, in one of his homilies at Naples with the help of a simple yet compelling image – that of the medicine which an individual, who is ill, feels obliged to accept on the advice of a doctor.

> We say to God, *Thy will be done*, in the same way as someone who is sick asks something from the physician: we take what he gives not exactly because we will it ourselves, but because it is the will of the physician; for if we only took what we ourselves willed, he would be fools. Hence we should ask nothing

---

15 Ibid.
16 Ibid.
17 Ibid.

of God save that His will be done in our regard; in other words that His will be fulfilled in us. Our hearts are only right when they are in accord with the divine will.[18]

Here the robust voice of the preacher is heard loud and clear. And, in order to further emphasize the point he wants to make, St Thomas, after a few moments, once again uses the image of the physician: 'God's will in our regard is that we keep His commandments, because when we desire something, we will not merely what we desire, but everything that will bring it about. Thus a physician, desiring to restore someone to a healthy condition, enjoins on that person a diet, medicine etc.'[19]

No one, to my knowledge, has remarked before now on the number of times St Thomas employs the image of sickness in these late sermons at Naples. On one occasion, for example, he remarks that a physician will sometimes refuse to apply 'violent remedies to a weak patient'.[20] And, on another occasion, he observes: 'human beings need counsel when they are in trouble, just as they need to consult a physician when they are sick. And so, when our souls are sick through sin, we must seek counsel so that we can be healed.'[21] The conferences at Naples were, we know, delivered towards the end of Thomas's life, at a time when he was no longer enjoying good health. Could that fact alone, perhaps, explain why the image of sickness occurs so often in these late sermons?

---

[18]   Ibid., No. 1061, p. 227.
[19]   Ibid., No. 1064, p. 228.
[20]   Ibid., No. 1102, p. 234.
[21]   Ibid., No. 1080, p. 231. In No. 1067, p. 228, we find two further brief references to physical infirmity.

6

'Give us this day our daily bread'

'Now perhaps some think it unfit for saints to seek from God bodily goods, and for this reason attribute a spiritual sense to these words. But, given that the chief concern of the saints should be to obtain spiritual gifts, it still becomes them to see that they seek, without blame, according to Our Lord's command, their common bread.'[1]

In contrast to the first three petitions of the Our Father, this fourth petition draws attention to some of our most basic and material human needs. 'Earlier the Lord had said "Hallowed be thy name" and "Thy will be done", wanting us to be heavenly in fulfilling God's will; but, mindful of our weakness, he now teaches us to ask also for the temporal things which are necessary to support life.'[2] Thomas makes this observation in

---

[1] St Cyril, cited by St Thomas in *Catena Aurea*, Lk. 11.1, p. 128.
[2] *The Lectures on St Matthew*, pp. 467–8. In one of the questions in the *Summa*, Thomas writes: 'The Lord's Prayer makes it abundantly clear that such petitions [ie requests for temporal goods] are not limited to eternal happiness; on the contrary, human beings have every right to hope for the good things of this life, temporal as well as spiritual.' This statement is not made, as it happens, in the body of the 'question', but forms part of an 'objection'. St Thomas, in his answer, explains that there is nothing

one of the lectures he gave on St Matthew's Gospel. Speaking at Naples in a similar vein, a few years later, he remarked: 'It is God who provides us with temporal goods. This is signified in the words *Give us this day our daily bread*.'[3] The desire to possess temporal goods, therefore, is something wholly natural. But, because of our fallen condition, St Thomas, when preaching at Naples, felt the need to warn his congregation about what he called 'the five sins which are usually committed out of a desire for temporal things'.[4]

1. 'The first is that inordinate desire whereby we seek for things which are beyond our state and condition of life.'[5] One of the examples Thomas gives is that of a priest who wants to dress up, not as an ordinary clergyman, but as a bishop! Thomas says, 'This vice draws a man away from spiritual things, in as much as it makes him have an overwhelming desire for things which are passing.'[6] But Christ, in teaching us the Our Father, instructed us to ask *for bread only*: 'He did not teach us to ask for delicacies, nor for many kinds of things, nor for what is over-refined, but for bread which is common to all, and without which human life cannot be sustained.'[7]

2. 'The second vice is that some people, in the acquisition of temporal goods, molest and defraud others, a practice

---

wrong with asking for temporal favours provided such favours in no way block the path to eternal happiness. All the temporal things we ask for in prayer should be ultimately subservient to that final beatitude. See ST, II II q. 17, a. 2, obj. 2 and ad 2.

[3] *In Orationem Dominicam*, No. 1071, p. 229. See 'Commentary on the Lord's Prayer,' p. 17.

[4] Ibid., No. 1072, p. 229.

[5] Ibid.

[6] Ibid.

[7] Ibid.

fraught with danger since it is difficult to restore ill-gotten goods.'[8] St Thomas quotes Augustine at this point: 'Sin is not forgiven until that which is taken away is restored.'[9] And so, Thomas continues, 'we are taught here to shun this vice, by asking for our own and not another's bread.'[10] But that is not all. In his Matthew Lectures Thomas reminds us that, if we are given temporal goods in sufficient abundance, these things 'should be accepted in such a way that we share them with others.' And then he adds this last tiny sentence from Job 31.17: 'I have not eaten my morsel of bread alone.'[11]

3. 'The third vice is excessive solicitude. There are some who are never content with what they have, but always want more: and this is a lack of moderation, since desire should always be measured according to one's needs: *Give me neither beggary nor riches, but give me only the necessities of life* (Prov. 30.8). We are warned to avoid this particular vice in the words, *Our daily bread*, that is to say, *the bread for one day or for one season*.'[12] St Thomas, in the Matthew Lectures, offers a thoughtful reflection on *Give us this day*, a phrase which might seem to indicate 'we ought to desire things one day at a time', and so forget about the future. Thomas states, on the contrary, 'the Lord did not intend to forbid people to take thought for the future, what he forbids is that we should not anticipate things by presuming to worry before it is time. If some concern is laid upon you now, that is what you should be worrying about, not something

---

[8] Ibid., No. 1073, pp. 229–30.
[9] Ibid., p. 230.
[10] Ibid.
[11] *The Lectures on St Matthew*, p. 468.
[12] *In Orationem Dominicam*, No. 1074, p. 230.

that may become your responsibility in the future.'[13]

4. 'The fourth vice is immoderate voraciousness. There are some who would devour in one day what would be sufficient for several days. These seek bread not for to-day but for ten days.'[14] Thomas, in his Matthew Lectures, notes that the word 'daily', in *Give us this day our daily bread*, is there to help prevent 'superfluity'.[15] It is directed, he says, 'against extravagant people who spend more on one dinner than would be necessary over many days'![16]

5. 'The fifth vice is ingratitude. A person grows proud in his riches, and does not recognize that what he has comes from God. This is a grave fault, for all the things we have, whether spiritual or temporal, come from God . . . Hence, in order to remove this vice, the prayer has *Give us* even *our daily bread*, to remind us that all we have comes from God.'[17]

* * *

Part of St Thomas's own prayer for 'daily bread' must have included, we may presume, a prayer for the things he needed in order to fulfil his demanding vocation as scholar and theologian. And Thomas may well have found himself repeating, on occasion, and with a certain urgency, a prayer of this kind. The sermon at Naples dealing with the petition, *Give us this day our daily bread*, opens with these words: 'It often happens that a person of great learning and wisdom becomes fearful and timid, and needs, as a result, fortitude of heart lest he

---

[13] *The Lectures on St Matthew*, pp. 469–70.
[14] *In Orationem Dominicam*, No. 1075, p. 230.
[15] *The Lectures on St Matthew*, p. 468. This statement and the one which follows are taken from L.
[16] Ibid.
[17] *In Orationem Dominicam*, No. 1076, p. 230.

lack necessities.'[18] But why, of all people on earth, should the wise and intelligent experience fear of this kind and, to such an extent, they require, in St Thomas's opinion, special grace and encouragement? Do Thomas's words betray, perhaps, something of his own individual fear of being deprived of all the things he knew he needed in order to respond well to the demands of his unique vocation? Whatever may be the answer to this question, St Thomas goes on at once to talk about the Spirit's gift of fortitude, which, he tells us, 'prevents man's heart from fainting through fear of lacking necessities, and makes him trust, without wavering, that God will provide him with all the things he needs.'[19]

*   *   *

The phrase 'our bread' in the prayer *Give us this day our daily bread*, can be interpreted, according to Thomas, in a number of different ways. It can be taken as referring simply to the basic necessities of life, to what he calls 'bodily bread'.[20] Or, it might be interpreted as referring to the Godhead itself, or to the divine precepts and commandments which Thomas calls 'the bread of wisdom'.[21] But, in the St Matthew Lectures, Thomas explains that it refers, first of all, to Christ, who said of himself: *I am the bread of life*, and to Christ, particularly, 'inasmuch as he is contained in the sacrament of the altar.'[22] This idea we find repeated in the conferences at Naples. There, Thomas explains that when we pray *Give us this day our daily bread*, we are asking

[18] Ibid., No. 1070, p. 229.
[19] Ibid. Notice, in passing, how sharp and telling is the link that Thomas makes here between asking for the basic necessities of life – the fourth petition – and the gift of fortitude.
[20] *The Lectures on St Matthew*, p. 467.
[21] Ibid.
[22] Ibid., p. 465.

for 'sacramental bread and for the bread of God's word.' We
are 'praying that, as we receive it in the Sacrament, it may profit
us unto salvation.'[23] Thomas then goes on to say: 'From this
we derive that happiness which is a hunger for justice. For the
possession of spiritual goods increases our desire for them, and
this desire arouses a hunger, and from this hunger there follows
abundance of everlasting life.'[24]

When we receive Christ as sacramental bread, we begin
already, in some measure, to experience the joy of eternal life.
What this means is that 'this day', in the prayer *Give us this day
our daily bread*, contains in itself already an eternal day, even
the promised day of resurrection. On this point, St Thomas
includes, in the *Catena Aurea*, the following remarkable text
from Pseudo-Augustine:

> It is not the [ordinary] bread which goes into the body, but
> the bread of everlasting life which gives support to the sub-
> stance of our soul . . . Take daily what profits you for the day,
> and so live that you may be worthy to receive. The death of
> the Lord is signified [by this bread], and the remission of sins.
> Whoever has a wound looks for medicine, and the wound is
> that we are under sin. The medicine is this heavenly and awe-
> some sacrament. If you receive daily, daily does 'Today' come
> to you. Christ is to you 'Today'. Christ rises to you daily.[25]

---

[23] *In Orationem Dominicam*, No. 1079, p. 230.
[24] Ibid. See ST, III q. 83, a. 4. Thomas notes that people are 'prepared for
communion' by reciting 'the common prayer of the congregation which
is the Lord's Prayer, in which we ask for our daily bread to be given us.'
[25] Pseudo-Augustine, cited by St Thomas in *Catena Aurea*, Lk. 11.1, p. 128.
The astonishing last three sentences of this text I have taken, with a few
small changes, from a translation of the *Catena Aurea* edited by John Henry
Newman. See *Catena Aurea: Commentary on the four Gospels culled out of the
writings of the Fathers by St Thomas Aquinas*, Vol III, St Luke (Southampton:
The Saint Austin Press, 1997; first published 1841) p. 389.

7

'And forgive us our trespasses as we forgive those who trespass against us'

'Here he begins to formulate the petitions which concern the taking away of evil, and he puts first the petition by which the single most important ill is taken away, namely guilt.'[1]

'[W]e all have some sin.'[2] This bald statement of fact occurs in one of the Lectures on Matthew's Gospel that St Thomas delivered at Paris. It is a statement intended to refute the naive notion that there are righteous people in this world who have no need of God's forgiveness since they have never committed even a single sin during their entire lives. 'But if this were the case,' Thomas notes, 'then there would be some people who could not say this prayer, whereas the Lord gave the prayer to all of us, and so we all have some sin. *The righteous will fall seven times a day* (Prov. 24.16). *For if we say that we have no sin, we deceive ourselves* (I John 1.8).'[3] On a related question, writing in the

[1] *The Lectures on St Matthew*, p. 470. This statement is taken from L.
[2] Ibid., pp. 470–1. Again, the phrase is taken from L.
[3] *The Lectures on St Matthew*, pp. 470–1. This sentence is taken from L. In the *Catena Aurea* (St Matthew) St Thomas includes the following

Summa, St Thomas takes issue with those people who imagine that, having already obtained the grace of the Holy Spirit, they can now do good and avoid sin without any further assistance of grace. But, of course, 'in the actual conditions of the state of human nature', the very opposite is the case.

> Although our nature is in fact healed as far as the spirit is concerned, it continues to be spoiled and infected as regards the flesh, through which it *serves the law of sin*, as Romans says. There remains also a kind of darkness of ignorance in the understanding, so that *we do not know what to pray for as we should*, as Romans again says. For because of the different ways in which things turn out, and because we do not even know ourselves perfectly, we cannot fully know what is for our good; thus *Wisdom* (9.14): *The thoughts of mortals are fearful, and our counsels uncertain.* And so we have to be directed and protected by God, who knows all things and can do all things. And for this reason even those who have been reborn, as sons and daughters of God by grace, fittingly pray, *And lead us not into temptation,* and, *Thy will be done on earth as it is in heaven,* and the other relevant parts of the Lord's Prayer.[4]

Although obviously a very brief prayer, the Our Father is, Thomas insists, a prayer of great power. In the first place, the words of the prayer can be invoked at a time of sickness for the sake of physical healing.[5] But of even more telling significance,

text from St Cyprian (*Tr.* vii. 15): 'How good and necessary it is for us to be reminded that we are sinners compelled to make petition for our offenses . . .!' And again: 'In order that no man may flatter himself with the pretence of innocence, and perish more wretchedly through self-exaltation, he is instructed that he commits sins every day by being instructed to pray for them.' *Catena Aurea*, Mt. 6.8, p. 84.
[4]   ST, I II q. 109, a. 9.
[5]   ST, II II q. 96, a. 4, obj. 1 and ad 1.

the recitation of the prayer can, according to Thomas, act as a powerful protection against spiritual evil. The Lord's Prayer, he writes, 'is to be said for protection not only against venial sins, but also against mortal sins.'[6] Reflecting at one point in the *Summa* about whether or not a prayer like the Our Father, when recited by a sinner, can win God's favour, Thomas replies: 'We obtain, by asking for them in prayer, things which we do not merit. For God hears even sinners when they ask for pardon for their sins . . . otherwise the publican would have prayed in vain, *God be merciful to me a sinner*, Luke 18.13.'[7] It is, therefore, humility in weakness – humility in the struggle against sin – and not pride in achievement, which wins God's favour. On this theme, in his *Catena Aurea*, Thomas includes the following sharp and illumined statement from St John Chrysostom: '[H]umility can uplift even a guilty man from the depths . . . [It] saved the Publican before the Pharisee, and led the Thief into paradise before the Apostles'![8]

* * *

The phrase *Forgive us our sins*, in the Lord's Prayer, reminds us of two of the basic things we need in Christian life: the first is to be humble, and the second is to be filled with hope.[9] Those men and women who are genuinely holy possess both of these characteristics, according to St Thomas. In marked contrast, however, there are others who seem to believe that human

[6] ST, I II q. 74, a. 8, ad 6. In what appears to be his first sermon at Naples, St Thomas, citing Augustine, remarks that one of the results of saying the Our Father is that 'venial sins are forgiven.' See *In Orationem Dominicam*, No. 1020, p. 221.

[7] ST, I II q. 114, a. 9, ad 1.

[8] St John Chrysostom (*Hom. De Prof. Ev.*), cited by St Thomas in *Catena Aurea*, Lk. 18.2, p. 196.

[9] See *In Orationem Dominicam*, Nos 1082–1083, p. 231.

beings, by their own strength, can avoid falling into sin. On this point, Thomas notes:

> [T]here have been some so presumptuous as to assert that we could live in this world and, by our own unaided strength, avoid sin. But this has been given to none save Christ, who had the Spirit beyond all measure, and the Blessed Virgin, who was full of grace and in whom there was no sin . . . To no other saint has this been granted without their incurring at least venial sin . . . And this is confirmed by this petition itself, for it cannot be doubted that it is fitting for even holy men and women to recite the *Our Father*, in which is contained the petition *Forgive us our debts*. And so all acknowledge and admit that they are sinners or debtors . . . The other thing is that we should ever live in hope, since though we are sinners we must not despair, lest despair lead us to various and greater sins . . . It is therefore most profitable for us to hope always since, however great a sinner a man may be, he should hope that God will forgive him provided he is thoroughly contrite and converted, and this hope is strengthened in us when we pray *Forgive us our debts*.[10]

* * *

With regard to the second part of the petition, 'as we forgive those who trespass against us,' Thomas remarked at Naples, and the statement is memorable: '[F]rom the moment a man desires God to be the Lord of all he does not avenge the injuries done to him, but leaves all that to God.'[11] A further comment, made during the St Matthew Lectures, underlines with equal force the need to show compassion. Thomas writes: 'It would

[10] Ibid., No. 1082, p. 231.
[11] Ibid., No. 1059, p. 227.

be outrageous for me to ask God for mercy and not grant mercy to my fellow servant.'[12] It is for this reason, Thomas goes on to explain, that the petition is made conditional. Only if we learn to forgive will we be forgiven. 'You might say: I will say the first part, *Forgive us . . .* but I will omit what follows, *As we forgive our debtors.* Would you seek to deceive Christ? You certainly do not deceive him. Christ who made this prayer remembers it well, and therefore he cannot be deceived. If, therefore, you say the words with your lips, fulfil them in your heart.'[13] Here, the conditional aspect of the prayer, though it may indeed appear, as St Thomas acknowledges, 'burdensome to some', is in fact both 'necessary' and 'profitable'.[14] It is profitable 'because by it we obtain the forgiveness of our sins', and necessary 'because without it there is no forgiveness of sins.' And Thomas adds: 'this is not surprising, because no sin can ever be forgiven without charity. *Charity covers all faults* (Luke 6.36).'[15] In the *Catena Aurea* St Thomas underlines this point with a telling sentence from St John Chrysostom: 'Considering these things, we ought to show mercy to our debtors. For they are to us, if we are wise, the cause of our greatest pardon.'[16]

On the subject of love of enemies, St Thomas echoes again and again the Gospel teaching about charity and forgiveness. But how, it might be asked, can you love someone who is acting towards you in a decidedly cruel and malicious manner? St Thomas confronts this question in his commentary on the *Sentences of Peter Lombard*, and his reply underlines the true basis of Christian love, how the kindness of authentic love is rooted

[12] *The Lectures on St Matthew*, p. 471.
[13] *In Orationem Dominicam*, No. 1068, p. 232.
[14] *The Lectures on St Matthew*, p. 474.
[15] Ibid., p. 474 and p. 475.
[16] St John Chrysostom, cited by St Thomas in *Catena Aurea*, Lk. 11.1, p. 129.

not merely in one's own subjective (hopefully graced) desire to be kind and good, but also in a certain *objective* quality possessed by one's neighbor – even if that neighbour happens to be an enemy – a quality which, when acknowledged, commands respect. Thomas writes: 'in evil people there are two things to be considered: the nature by which they are men, and the malice by which they are evil. Since by their nature they bear in themselves the image of God and are capable of receiving divine life, they are therefore to be loved from charity according to that nature. Their malice, however, is contrary to divine life, and it is therefore to be hated in them.'[17]

Charity – supernatural charity – offers a perspective that is not available at the level of mere nature, and it is a truly saving perspective. St Thomas writes: 'Now there are some people in this life who seem incurably bad if mere human powers are taken into account, and yet are not really incurable if one takes into account the order of divine mercy by which they can be rescued . . . Now charity looks to what is divine, whereas [natural] friendship looks to what is human.'[18] Friendships of the natural order may, St Thomas acknowledges, be severed for one reason

---

[17] *Scriptum super libros Sententiarum*, Bk 3, Dist. 28, a. 4. See *On Love and Charity: Readings from the Commentary on the Sentences of Peter Lombard*, trans. P. A. Kwasniewski (Washington: The University of America Press, 2008) p. 192. Writing later in the *Sentences*, St Thomas remarked: '[W]e are bound to love someone according as he shares something in common with us. Now our enemy has in common with us a sharing in human nature, on the basis of which it is possible for him to have in common with us a sharing in the divine life. Accordingly, we ought to love him in regard to things that pertain to his nature and to the possession of grace, whereas we ought not to love the enmity he has against us, since according to it he has something in common neither with us nor even with himself, but rather something that is contrary [both to us and to himself].' Ibid., BK 3, Dist. 30, a. 1, ad 1; *On Love and Charity*, p. 245.

[18] Ibid., Bk 3, Dist. 28, a. 5; *On Love and Charity*, p. 194.

or another. But, in marked contrast, he insists, 'charity is not broken off with *anyone* in this life.'[19] How, in practice, to react to the deliberate malice of certain people was, at this point in his life, by no means a merely theoretical question for St Thomas. James Weisheipl writes: 'Thomas's four years of lecturing on the *Sentences* were turbulent years beset with many vicissitudes arising from the anti-mendicant controversy . . . The scene was hostile from the very day Thomas arrived in Paris.'[20]

Another question arises at this point: what can we say of the individual, man or woman, who finds it impossible to forgive a particular enemy who has been the cause of some deep hurt? Can that person, when praying the Lord's Prayer, presume to recite the phrase, 'as we forgive those who trespass against us'? The obvious reply would seem to be, 'Surely not, since the words when spoken would be a lie.' But that, as it happens, is not the answer St Thomas gives. And his reply, though brief, is particularly helpful and illuminating. For, with one quiet statement, it casts light on the underlying *ecclesial* character of all Christian prayer. St Thomas declares, 'I answer that he [or she] does not lie, for he is praying not in his own person, but *in that of the Church.*'[21] The *Pater Noster*, although clearly a prayer which can be said by an individual Christian praying in solitude, is never merely a private event of the spirit, a grace in isolation, but *always* an act of communion with others, an event of grace *in medio ecclesiae.* Thus, even if the prayer happens to be said by someone who has not yet been able or willing to forgive offences, it is still basically valid. Thomas explains, 'The prayer is pronounced, not in the name of the individual, but in the name

---

[19] Ibid.
[20] James Weisheipl, *Friar Thomas d'Aquino: His Life, Thought and Works* (Washington: The Catholic University of America Press, 1983) p. 67.
[21] *In Orationem Dominicam*, No. 1090, p. 232. Italics mine.

of the whole Church, and there is no doubt that the Church forgives the debts of all those who are in the Church.'[22]

*   *   *

Of course, it is one thing to forgive one's enemies, but are we expected also to *pray* for our enemies? Thomas addresses this question in Question 83 of the second part of the *Summa*, and allows us to hear, at one point, in the form of one or two objections, the tough voice of what might sound, at first hearing, like robust common sense. Since war, on occasion, is regarded as necessary, and since 'sometimes we lawfully fight against our enemies', then it would seem clear that 'we should not pray for our enemies'.[23] The statement is direct and unambiguous, but there is another statement (also in the form of an objection) that goes even further, declaring: 'we ought not to pray for our enemies, we ought to pray against them'![24] Responding to these hard and strong voices, St Thomas makes the following calm reply: 'we are bound to pray for our enemies in the same way that we are bound to love them . . . we must love their human nature, not their guilt.'[25] This does not mean, of course, that we are forbidden in every circumstance to take up arms against our enemies. What it does mean is that, on the occasion of a just war, for example, our own involvement in the struggle will, at core, represent a willingness and determination

---

[22] *The Lectures on St Matthew*, p. 472. In the *Summa* Thomas writes: 'The Lord's Prayer is offered in the name [literally 'in the common person'] of the whole Church. Therefore, if anyone says the prayer while unwilling to forgive a neighbour, that person does not lie. Although the words are not true for him personally, they are true as referred to the Church as a whole.' ST, II II q. 83, a. 16, ad 3.

[23] ST, II II q. 83 a. 8, obj. 3.

[24] ST, II II q. 83, a. 8, obj. 2.

[25] ST, II II q. 83, a. 8.

to prevent our enemies from committing further sin.[26]

Not everyone today, I suspect, will be at one with St Thomas's thinking on this subject. A majority may well be surprised, even shocked, to discover that, in the opinion of Thomas, we are *not* directly commanded in the Gospel to pray for our individual enemy, but merely commanded to pray for enemies *in general*.[27] St Thomas regards praying for one's most immediate enemy as a practice that is, needless to say, profoundly Christian. But, according to his understanding, it is not a matter of precept, something which has been actually *commanded* by God, and expected *here and now* of each and every Christian whatever their strength or weakness. It is rather a practice normally undertaken by people who have already attained to a significant degree of holiness. It is, in short, 'a work of perfection'.[28]

This statement does not mean that the average Christian should feel justified in taking up a fixed and complacent *minimalist* position with regard to love of enemy. Some people, however, after reading Aquinas, might just be inclined to make that mistake. And probably for that reason the Dominican theologian, Servais Pinckaers, felt it necessary to point out that 'the virtue of charity possesses an interior dynamism which carries it towards progress and towards a certain perfection'.[29] He writes: 'one cannot merely hold to what is of precept [viz. the com-

---

[26] ST, II II q. 83, a. 8, ad 3.
[27] ST, II II q. 83, a. 8.
[28] In the *Sentences* St Thomas writes: 'loving enemies to the extent of showing benevolence to them belongs to perfection, and not all are bound to do this. But to desire for one's enemy that he receive God's grace and inherit eternal life, which is charity's special concern, is something everyone is bound to do.' *Scriptum super libros Sententiarum*, Bk 3, Dist. 30, a. 1, ad 1. See *On Love and Charity: Readings from the Commentary on the Sentences of Peter Lombard*, p. 246.
[29] Servais Pinckaers, *La Prière Chrétienne* (Freiburg: Éditions Universitaires, 1989) p. 250.

mand to love enemies *in general*] as to a sufficient minimum, and refuse to go forward, using the pretext that progress of that kind is reserved for the perfect and the saints.'[30]

One of the most astonishing sentences in all of St Thomas's theological work occurs in Question 83 of the second part of the *Summa*. There, the saint goes so far as to suggest that 'it is lawful, when at prayer, to ask that some temporal evils befall our enemies so that they might mend their ways'![31] This statement, although astonishing in itself, is not in fact unique in Thomas's writing. Years earlier, in his commentary on the *Sentences*, he had written: 'someone can, while preserving charity, desire temporal evil for another person . . . but not precisely *as* that person's evil, but rather as an evil that prevents other evils from occurring.'[32] Later, in the same text, he goes on to note: 'Something similar can be said about [desiring] the evil of someone who falls into temporal evil, insofar as the evil of punishment frequently impedes the evil of [further] guilt on his part.'[33]

These statements of Aquinas need to be read with very particular care. I say this because, at first hearing, they sound like a distinct lowering of the Christian call to forgiveness, an invitation even to practice the very opposite of charity. But once the texts have been read with attentiveness and understanding, it soon becomes clear that the ideal of charity has not for a moment been ignored or set aside. It is still there in all its purity and challenge. St Thomas, as a spiritual guide and theologian, refuses to forget that the vast majority of people within the Church are very far from perfection, and that not many

[30] Ibid.
[31] ST, II II q. 83 a. 8, ad 3.
[32] *Scriptum super libros Sententiarum*, Bk 3, Dist. 30, a. 6. See *On Love and Charity: Readings from the Commentary on the Sentences of Peter Lombard*, p. 246.
[33] Ibid.

are capable, here and now, of manifesting heroic generosity or saintly benevolence towards their persecutors. That's why, with regard to the ideal of *caritas*, St Thomas is determined to keep his feet firmly planted on the ground. His words, both here in the *Summa* and elsewhere, though always imbued with Christian hope, are never tainted by naïve optimism. Certainly, they reflect the strength and challenge of the Gospel, but they manifest also an eminently wise and practical and compassionate understanding of human character and human psychology.

8

'And lead us not into temptation'

'God would have us pray to him that we may not be led into temptation, though he could have done this for us without our prayer, but he wanted us to be made aware from whom we receive all benefits.' [1]

What does this petition mean? Can it really be possible that God in some way wants to tempt us? Is God somehow involved in the actual process of temptation? Is the nature of God really that complicated? *Lead us not into temptation* – this short phrase – was cited by Carl Gustav Jung in a remarkable memoir in which he recalled the moment when, as a young man, he came to the unhappy and mistaken conviction that God was not only 'love and goodness', but was also the very opposite of goodness, a decidedly evil and frightening phenomenon. Jung did not hesitate to call God 'the tempter and destroyer'. [2]

---

[1]   St Augustine (*De Don. Pers. 5*), cited by St Thomas in *Catena Aurea*, Mt. 6.9, p. 85.
[2]   See Carl Gustav Jung, *Memories, Dreams, Reflections*, recorded and edited by Aniela Jaffé, trans. R. and C. Winston (New York: Vintage Books, 1963) p. 56.

When St Thomas addresses this question in the Sermon-Conferences at Naples, he declares: 'no man is tempted by God, for it is said, *God cannot be tempted to evil things, and he does not tempt anybody* (James 1.13).'[3] Sometimes, however, our virtue is tested in the matter of avoiding evil, not because such virtue is unknown to God but 'in order that all might know it and take it as an example'.[4] But if God is not tempting us, by whom, then, or by what, are we tempted? The answer Thomas gives is the answer which is given in the New Testament. We are tempted by three things: 'by the flesh, by the devil, and by the world.'[5]

First: 'We are tempted by the *flesh* . . . because the flesh incites us to evil, inasmuch as it always seeks its own gratification, namely carnal pleasures in which sin often occurs. For those who indulge in carnal pleasures neglect spiritual things . . . *Everyone is tempted . . . by his own lust* (James I:14).'[6] And Thomas continues: 'the spirit for its part would delight always in spiritual goods, but the flesh, asserting itself, hinders the spirit: *The corruptible body is a load upon the soul* (Wisdom 60.15).'[7] Thomas then quotes the famous text from Romans: '*I delight in the law of God after the inward man, but I behold another law in my members, warring against the law of my mind, and making me a captive to the law of sin which is in my members* (Rom 7.22, 23).'[8]

Second: the *world* tempts us, and in fairly obvious ways, by love of money, for example, and by 'an excessive and unbridled desire for temporal goods'.[9] Third: the *devil* tempts us,

---

[3]   *In Orationem Dominicam*, No. 1094, p. 233. Italics mine.
[4]   Ibid., No. 1093, p. 233.
[5]   Ibid., No. 1094, p. 233.
[6]   Ibid., No. 1095, p. 233.
[7]   Ibid.
[8]   Ibid.
[9]   Ibid., No. 1098, p. 233.

but tempts us, Thomas points out, 'most cunningly'.[10] Against
the devil we have 'a mighty struggle': '*Our wrestling is not against
flesh and blood, but against principalities and powers, against the
rulers of the world of this darkness, against the spirits of wickedness in
high places.* (Eph 6.12).'[11] The devil, Thomas then goes on to
note, 'seeks out the weak places in the object of his assault; he
tempts us in the area in which he sees us to be most weak.'[12]
And, what is more, he does not propose to us 'something that
has an appearance of evil but something that has a semblance
of good.'[13] This temptation will most often attack those who
have already made significant progress in the spiritual life.
Yielding no longer now to the sins of the flesh, they can become
vulnerable to what Thomas calls 'spiritual sins' such as 'anger'
and 'pride', and these are more serious sins.[14] (St Thomas, in
his 'commentary' on the Ten Commandments, remarks: 'Sins
of the flesh are shameful – they are "*infamiae*" – but sins of the
flesh are less culpable than sins of the spirit.'[15])

One might be inclined to think, after this brief reflection
on the subject, that temptation, both in its inception and in
its fruit, is somehow always evil. But St Thomas says something
at this point which is rather unexpected: 'Christ teaches us to
pray not that we may not be tempted, but that we may not be
led into temptation. For it is when one overcomes temptation
that one deserves a crown.'[16] Accordingly, when we recite the
phrase *Lead us not into temptation*, we are not asking God that we

---

[10] Ibid., No. 1096, p. 233.

[11] Ibid.

[12] Ibid.

[13] Ibid., No. 1097, p. 233.

[14] Ibid., No. 1096, p. 233.

[15] St Thomas Aquinas, *In duo praecepta caritatis et in decem legis praecepta
expositio*, No. 1287, in *Opuscula theologica*, Vol 2, *De re spirituali*, Marietti
edition (Rome: 1954) p. 266.

[16] *In Orationem Dominicam*, No. 1099, p. 233.

might never again be tempted. For temptation, Thomas insists, is 'useful': 'People are tempted so that they may become known to themselves and to other people.'[17] Only in that sense can we speak of God tempting us.

> In this way God tempted Abraham and Job also, and it is thus that he often sends trials to the righteous so that, by putting up with trials patiently, they will make manifest their virtue, and also make progress themselves in virtue: *The Lord your God tests you so that it may appear whether or not you love him* (Deutr 13.3). Thus God tempts us by inciting us to good deeds.[18]

In contemporary spirituality it is almost a commonplace to think of the spiritual or the mystical life as a way of coming to experience God. But, in Sacred Scripture, as the texts cited above would seem to indicate, what is of far greater importance is what we might call God's experience of us, God's testing of us, God's thirst for our attention and our love. St Thomas, in his commentary on Psalm 16, writes: 'When God examines, he does three things, namely, he tests, he visits, he examines.'[19] What is more, as a result of this testing, as soon as God finds that an individual possesses a certain integrity, there begins the deeper testing, the more searching examination. Thomas cites Jer. 17.10: *I, the Lord, search the heart and probe the loins. I give everyone according to his way.*[20] Finding oneself under this kind of mysterious, divine scrutiny is a wonderful sign of grace and of progress in the spiritual life. But the experience itself is not

---

[17] *The Lectures on St Matthew*, p. 473.
[18] *In Orationem Dominicam*, No. 1093, p. 233.
[19] Psalm 16, *In psalmos Davidis expositio*, in *Sancti Thomae Aquinatis opera omnia*, Parma edition, Vol 14, p. 190.
[20] Ibid.

'wonderful'. Thomas notes: 'this examination is severe and strong, and so much so that no one would withstand it unless helped by God.'[21]

Here, St Thomas's way of speaking about the spiritual life recalls, in some measure, the vivid language St John of the Cross uses in his work when attempting to describe the experience of the dark night of purification. So can we say, therefore, that St Thomas is of one mind on this subject with the Carmelite mystic? Does the Dominican really believe our human nature is such that it requires this sort of radical transformation? Is he not the theologian who famously declared that grace does not destroy nature but rather perfects it? Well, St Thomas is indeed the great Christian humanist who made this declaration. But we must be careful not to glide too quickly, or too easily, over what is involved, in practice, in the *perfecting* of our nature, and forget or deliberately ignore how purifying and demanding that process can be.

When St Thomas, in the text we have been considering, comes to describe the experience of being tested, he uses the same images that we find repeated over and over again in the work of St John of the Cross, namely night and fire. Commenting on the phrase, '*Visitasti nocte, You have visited me by night*', Thomas notes: 'This visitation can be understood by night and fire because both disturb the soul. (Job 30.17) *By night my bone is pierced with sorrows: and fire does the same.*'[22] In the end, what the examination by fire demonstrates is, according to Thomas, 'whether or not the person [undergoing the trial] is a true friend [*bonus amicus*], someone who does not withdraw.'[23]

---

[21] Ibid.
[22] Ibid.
[23] Ibid.

9

'But deliver us from evil'

'We ought to pray not only that we may not be led into evil from which we are free [at present], but that we may be set free from that evil into which we have already been led. Therefore, it follows, Deliver us from evil.'[1]

'This,' Thomas says, 'is the last petition.' It is a prayer for deliverance 'from past, present, and future evil, from the evil of guilt, of punishment and of all ill.'[2] Here, Thomas has in mind not only the evil of sin and its consequences, but also the many other different kinds of trouble and affliction we endure such as sicknesses or hurts inflicted on us by our enemies. But now the question: will God answer us when we pray to him for deliverance? Thomas replies in the affirmative. In the Naples conferences he lists four of the ways in which we can hope to be liberated from present trials and afflictions.

1. First, he says, there are times when God directly intervenes to prevent their occurrence. 'But this is rare; for the saints are afflicted in this world, *since everyone who would live*

---

[1] St Augustine (*De Don. Pers.* 5), cited by St Thomas in *Catena Aurea*, Mt. 6.10, p. 85.
[2] *The Lectures on St Matthew*, p. 473

piously in Christ Jesus shall suffer persecution' (2 Tim. 3.12).[3] Then Thomas qualifies this statement a little, noting: 'sometimes God does prevent us from being afflicted by an evil, that is, when he knows we are weak, and unable to bear it. Just so a physician prescribes violent remedies to a weak patient.'[4]

2. The second way of deliverance refers not to the actual removal of affliction but rather to the comfort God gives us in the midst of affliction, 'for unless he consoles us, we cannot hold out.'[5] Thomas then quotes two short sentences from St Paul's Second Letter to the Corinthians: *We were utterly weighed down beyond our strength* (2 Cor. I.8), and again: *God who comforts the humble, comforts us* (2 Cor. 7.6).[6] In his own commentary on the Second Letter to the Corinthians, Thomas explains why St Paul calls God 'the Father of Mercies' and 'the God of all comfort': '[Paul] thanks God for the two things human beings particularly need: first, to have evil removed from them, and this is done by mercy which takes away misery, for it is a characteristic of a father to have compassion . . . Secondly, they need to be supported in the face of evils which occur, and that is to receive comfort. Because, unless we have something on which our hearts can rest, we will not be able to stand firm when evils come down on us. A person comforts another by affording that other person something refreshing in which to rest in evil times. And though an individual might be comforted by something, and find rest, and be supported by it, in the case of certain evils, it is God alone who comforts us in all evils. And so [Paul] calls him the

[3] *In Orationem Dominicam*, No. 1102, p. 234.
[4] Ibid.
[5] Ibid., No. 1103, p. 234.
[6] Ibid.

God of all comfort, for if you sin God comforts you since he is merciful.'[7]

3. With regard to the third way of deliverance, Thomas has in mind the 'many blessings' which are sometimes bestowed on those in affliction, blessings so great and so many the original evil they suffered is completely forgotten. Again, Thomas quotes, at this point, from 2 Corinthians: *For that which is at present momentary and light, in terms of our affliction, is working for us, and in a way beyond all measure, an eternal weight of glory'* (2 Cor. 4.17).[8]

4. What St Thomas proposes as the fourth and final form of deliverance is a truly shocking paradox. For, here, the very trials and tribulations themselves are regarded as the bearers of deliverance, things 'conducive to our good'.[9] Thus, 'He [Jesus] did not say *Deliver us from tribulation,* but *from evil* because tribulations bring the saints a crown, and for that reason they glory in their trials.'[10]

Among the most famous examples in the New Testament of the workings of grace in this regard, perhaps the most striking is the 'sting' or 'thorn' in the flesh of St Paul, which so greatly troubled the Apostle. St Thomas, in his Naples discourse on the Our Father, draws our attention to the text in 2 Corinthians where Paul speaks on the subject, 2 Cor. 12.8-9: '*Three times I besought the Lord about this, that it should leave me, but he said to me, "My grace is sufficient for you, for my power is made perfect in weakness." I will all the more gladly boast of my weakness, that the power of Christ may rest*

---

[7]   St Thomas Aquinas, *In epistolam 2 ad Corinthios,* ch. I, 2, in *Sancti Thomae Aquinatis opera omnia,* Parma edition, Vol 13, p. 301.

[8]   *In Orationem Dominicam,* No. 1104, p. 234.

[9]   Ibid., No. 1105, p. 234.

[10]   Ibid.

upon me.'[11] In St Thomas's own commentary on 2 Corinthians, there is an extended reflection on the subject of St Paul's 'thorn in the flesh', and on the seeming failure of the saint's prayer for deliverance (2 Cor. 12.7-9). The passage is of such immediate relevance to the final petition of the Our Father, *Deliver us from evil*, and is so intrinsically interesting in itself, I have decided to quote it here at considerable length:

> [V]ery often a wise physician procures and permits a lesser disease to come over a person in order to cure or avoid a greater one. Thus, to cure a spasm he procures a fever. This, the Apostle shows was done to him by the Physician of souls, our Lord Jesus Christ. For Christ, as the supreme Physician of souls, by way of curing grave spiritual faults, permits many of his great elect to be gravely afflicted by physical sickness. And, what's more, to cure [or prevent] greater sins [*crimina*], he permits them to fall into lesser and even mortal sins. But, among all the sins the gravest is pride . . . pride is an inordinate desire for one's own excellence. For if an individual seeks some excellence under God, and seeks it moderately and for a good end, it can be sustained. But, if it is not done with due order, that individual can even fall into other vices, such as ambition, avarice, vainglory and the like . . . Therefore, because the matter of this vice, that is pride, is mainly found in things that are good, because its matter is something good, God sometimes permits his elect to be prevented by something on their part (e.g. infirmity or some other defect, and sometimes even mortal sin) from obtaining such a good, in order that they be so humbled on this account that they will not take pride in it, and that being thus humiliated they may recognize that they cannot stand

[11] Ibid., No. 1026, p. 222.

by their own powers . . . Therefore, because the Apostle had good reason for glorying in his spiritual election . . . given the outstanding knowledge with which he shone and which especially puffs one up: for this reason the Lord applied a remedy lest he be elated with pride. And this is what he says: *to keep me from being too elated by the abundance of revelations . . . a thorn was given me*, i.e. for my benefit and humiliation: *You have lifted me up and set me, as it were, upon the wind* (Job 31.22); there was given to me, I say, a thorn tormenting my body with bodily weakness that the soul might be healed. For it is said that he literally suffered a great deal from pain in the *eleum* [pelvis]. Or *a thorn in the flesh*, i.e. of concupiscence arising from my flesh, by which he was greatly troubled: *For I do not do the good I want, but the evil I do not want is what I do . . . So, then, I of myself serve the law of God with my mind, but with my flesh I serve the law of sin* (Rom 7.19, 25).[12]

At this point Thomas takes up once again the image of the physician in order to explain why the thorn in the flesh of St Paul was necessary for him as a man and an Apostle, and was even somehow, at the end, by God's grace, an occasion of great blessing.

Now the Apostle was understandably anxious to have this thorn removed, and prayed that it might be removed . . . Note here the way a sick person, ignorant of the reason why a physician supplies a stinging plaster, asks the physician to remove it . . . Likewise, the Apostle, feeling that the sting was too painful for him, sought help from the unique Physician to have it removed . . . But the Lord said to me: *my grace is sufficient for you*. As if to say: it is not necessary that

---

[12] *In epistolam 2 ad Corinthios*, ch. XIII, 3, p. 371.

this bodily weakness leave you, because it is not dangerous, since you will not be led into impatience, because my grace strengthens you. And nor is it necessary that this weakness of concupiscence be removed, because it will not lead you into sin, since my grace will protect you . . . Thus, a medicine, inasmuch as it is bitter should be avoided. Yet, when it is considered in relation to health, a person [naturally] seeks it. Therefore, a thorn in the flesh, by itself, is to be avoided as troublesome, but inasmuch as it is a means to virtue, and an exercise of virtue, it should be desired. The Apostle, since the secret of divine providence had not yet been revealed to him (namely, that it would turn out to his advantage) considered that, in itself, it was something bad for him. But God, who had ordained this for the good of his humility, did not give in to what he wished. Once, however, the matter was understood, the Apostle afterwards gloried in it, saying *I will all the more gladly boast of my weaknesses, that the power of Christ may rest upon me.*[13]

The fourth way in which God 'delivers' us from evil, as evidenced here in the life of St Paul, is a form of liberation which is – to say the least – paradoxical. St Thomas writes: 'God delivers us from evil and from trials', not by immediately removing the evil or rescuing us from the trials in this life, but 'by turning them to our profit.' And he adds: 'it is a mark of wisdom to direct evil to good, and this is the result of patience in bearing trials. Other virtues operate by good things, but patience profits by evil things.'[14] St Thomas made this particular comment during what appears to be his final sermon at Naples on the Our Father. And it is significant that, when he came to speak

[13] Ibid., Ch. 12, 3, pp. 371–2.
[14] *In Orationem Dominicam*, No. 1105, pp. 234–5.

on that occasion of how 'temptations and trials are conducive to our profit', and how the saints learn to 'glory in their trials', he pointed at once, and uniquely, to the example of St Paul: 'Thus the Apostle says (Rom 5.3): *More than that, we glory in our tribulations, knowing that tribulation brings patience.*'[15]

* * *

The petitions of the Our Father conclude with the prayer, *Deliver us from evil.* And for Thomas, there could be no finer or more suitable end to the *Pater Noster.* Accordingly, in the *Catena Aurea* he cites the following passage from St Cyprian:

> After all these preceeding petitions, at the conclusion of the prayer comes a sentence, comprising briefly and collectively all our petitions and desires. For there remains nothing beyond for us to ask for, after petition has been made for God's protection from evil. For, that gained, we are secure against all the things that the devil and the world can work against us. For what has one to fear from this life when one has God, all through life, as one's guardian?'[16]

The spirit of confidence evident in this text of Cyprian is something which characterizes all of Aquinas's reflections on the final petition of the Our Father. But one shadow still remains, and it is a reality which Thomas never allows himself to forget. Yes, it is true that we are, by God's grace, ultimately protected in this life from the damage which evil can wreck upon our spirit. But, in one form or other, evil will be oppressing us as long as we are alive in this world. And that is why we find St Thomas,

---

[15] Ibid., p. 234.
[16] St Cyprian (*Tr.* vii. 18), cited by St Thomas in *Catena Aurea*, Mt. 6.10, p. 85.

95

in his writings, looking forward with such deep longing for that eternal life in heaven where evil will have finally lost all its power. He writes:

> [T]he presence of all good requires the utter banishment of evil . . . In that final state of good, therefore, those who possess all good will not only have a perfect sufficiency, but they will enjoy complete serenity and security as a result of their freedom from evil, according to Proverbs 1.33: *Whoever will listen to me will rest free from terror, and will enjoy abundance without fear of evils.* A further result is that absolute peace will reign in heaven. [Here] our peace is blocked either by the inner restlessness of desire (when we covet what as yet we don't possess) or by the irksomeness of certain evils which we suffer or fear that we may suffer. But in heaven there is nothing to fear. Restlessness of craving will end, because of the full possession of all good. Every external cause of disturbance will cease, because all evil will be absent. The perfect tranquility of peace will be enjoyed there. Isaiah 32.18 alludes to this: *My people shall sit in the beauty of peace* (i.e., the perfection of peace). To show the cause of peace the prophet adds the phrase *And in the tabernacles of confidence,* since confidence will reign when the fear of evil is abolished.[17]

---

[17] *Compendium theologiae,* 9, pp. 203–4; Vollert, pp. 363–4.

10

'Amen'

'Amen, which appears here at the end, affirms what has been written, and is the seal of the Lord's Prayer.'[1]

The Our Father concludes with the word 'Amen'. By this word Amen, Thomas declares in one of his *Lectures on St Matthew*, 'We are given confidence that we shall obtain what we pray for.'[2] And, again, in the same commentary, he cites this brief, encouraging statement from Heb. 4.16: 'Let us approach with confidence to the throne of grace.'[3] *Confidence* – that is the one word which, like a vivid thread, runs from beginning to end throughout all of St Thomas's reflections on the Our Father. The prayer itself is, of course, manifestly short. But, being short, it is able, Thomas notes, 'to give us confidence that we shall easily obtain what we are asking for.'[4] What's more, it is a prayer of great simplicity. There is nothing whatever esoteric about it: 'everyone can easily

---

[1]   St Jerome, cited by St Thomas in *Catena Aurea*, Mt. 6.10, p. 85.
[2]   *The Lectures on St Matthew*, p. 474.
[3]   Ibid., p. 455.
[4]   Ibid., p. 455. In one of the texts included by St Thomas in the *Catena Aurea* (Mt. 6.3) we read: 'Among the divine and saving instructions by which he [Christ Jesus] counsels believers, he proposed and set forth for us a form of prayer in few words, thus giving us confidence our prayer would be granted quickly and, for that reason, he desires that we pray briefly.' See *Catena Aurea* (*Gloss.e.Cypr*), p. 81.

learn it, both great and small, learned and unlearned . . . *The Lord will make a shortened word upon the earth* (Is. 10.23).'[5]

So efficacious is the Lord's Prayer, and so surprisingly inclusive in what it embraces, that St Thomas does not hesitate to declare that 'anything that can be contained in other prayers is contained in this one.'[6] He writes: 'The Lord directed human intention by a short prayer, in which he taught us how to pray, and showed us what we should hope for, and what should be our aim.'[7] Once, when preaching to the people at Naples, he spoke about the 'three-fold good', which is achieved by all authentic prayer, and achieved most especially, therefore, by the Lord's Prayer. His words were direct and to the point, and his basic message to the people so encouraging in its import, and so comprehensive in its range of reference, the passage deserves, I am persuaded, to be cited here in full.

> In the first place prayer is an efficacious and useful remedy against evils. Thus it delivers us from sins already committed: *You have forgiven the wickedness of my sin, and for this let every good man pray to you* (Psalm 31.5,6). Thus the Thief on his cross prayed, and obtained pardon: *This day you shall be with me in paradise* (Luke 23.43). Thus also prayed the Publican, and *went down to his house justified* (ibid., 18.14). Prayer also frees us from the fear of future sin, and from trials and despondency: *Is any one of you sad? Let him pray* (James 5.13). Again, it delivers us from persecutors and enemies: *Instead of making me a return of love, they disparaged me; but I gave myself to prayer* (Psalm 108.4). Secondly, prayer is efficacious and useful for obtaining all that we desire: *All things whatsoever you ask, when*

[5] Ibid.
[6] 'The Lectures on St Matthew,' p. 455.
[7] *Compendium theologiae (De Fide)* I, p. 83; see *Compendium of Theology*, trans., R. J. Regan, p. 17.

you pray, believe that you shall receive (Mark 11.24). And if our prayer is not granted, it is either because we do not persevere in prayer, *whereas we ought always to pray and not to faint* (Luke 18.1), or because we do not ask for that which is more conducive to our salvation. Thus Augustine says: *Often our good Lord does not give us what we want so as to give us what we really would prefer.* We have an example of this in Paul who three times prayed for the removal of the sting in his flesh, and yet was not heard (2 Cor 12.8,9). Thirdly, prayer is profitable in as much as it makes us the familiars of God.[8]

That last statement is remarkable. By reciting the Lord's Prayer we, in some way, become the friends of God. The simple fact of talking to the Lord, and using his own words, indicates that the prayer we are saying is that of 'an intimate and devoted friend.'[9] Having made that observation, it is surely not surprising that St Thomas, in the very next sentence, could go on to declare: 'this prayer is never fruitless.'[10]

*   *   *

At core, the Our Father is a humble prayer of petition, and indeed of *insistent* petition. But it is also, St Thomas is concerned to remind us, a prayer which allows us to engage in direct and intimate dialogue with God. A conversation, in other words, between friends. 'Consider what a joy is granted you, to talk with God in your prayers, asking for whatever you want, whatever you desire.'[11] Cited twice in the work of Aquinas, this

---

[8]   *In Orationem Dominicam,* Nos 1025–1027, p. 222.
[9]   Ibid., No. 1020, p. 221. Here Thomas is echoing a statement made by St Cyprian (*De Orat. Dom.*).
[10] Ibid.
[11] On the question of friendship in St Thomas, see Daniel Schwartz, *Aquinas on Friendship* (Oxford: Oxford University Press, 2007).

statement was originally attributed, in the ancient tradition, to
St John Chrysostom. St Thomas includes it in both the Lucan
Catena Aurea,[12] and also in Question 83 of the *Summa*.[13] One
can well imagine how greatly it must have impressed him. But
no less impressive, I would suggest, is the following brief text
from St Thomas himself, taken from the last treatise he wrote
on the Our Father. Because the passage marks a fitting end to
our reflections so far, I have thought it wise to let these few,
contemplative words of Aquinas – words instinct with living
knowledge of God and with a wonderful hope – bring to a close
the present study:

> [W]hen we pray to God, the very prayer we send forth makes
> us intimate with him, inasmuch as our soul is raised up to
> God, converses with him in spiritual affection, and adores
> him in spirit and truth. This affectionate intimacy, experi-
> enced in prayer, prepares a way to return to prayer with even
> greater confidence.[14]

[12] St John Chrysostom, cited by St Thomas in *Catena Aurea*, Lk. 18.1,
p. 194.
[13] See ST, II II q. 83, a. 2, ad 3. The *Summa* version is slightly different:
'Consider what a joy is granted to you, what glory is given you, to talk
with God in your prayers, to converse with Christ, asking for whatever
you want, whatever you desire.'
[14] *Compendium theologiae*, 2, p. 194.

Appendix

CHARACTER AND HISTORY OF AQUINAS'S TEXTS ON THE OUR FATHER

1. *'Our Father' in the* Commentary on the Sentences

St Thomas first gave attention to the nature and character of the Lord's Prayer in what was, in fact, the first major theological work of his career, his commentary on the *Sentences of Peter Lombard*. This commentary, consisting of four quite lengthy books, was composed in Paris between the years 1252–56. At one point in the work, the entire focus of St Thomas's attention is on the relationship between the seven petitions in the prayer and the gifts of the Holy Spirit (Book III, distinction 34, q. 1, a. 6). Here, as elsewhere in Thomas's reflections on the Our Father, St Augustine of Hippo is the major influence.

2. *'Our Father' in the* Catena Aurea (*St Matthew*)

Sometime after he returned from Paris to Italy in 1259, St Thomas was assigned as lector to Orvieto. And, during the time he was there, at the request of his friend, Pope Urban IV, he undertook to compose an extended gloss or commentary on all four Gospels. It was an enormous undertaking, the actual texts of this 'continuous exposition' being culled from a vast range of both eastern and western patristic sources.[1] The particular gloss on St Matthew, including the various quotations regarding the Lord's Prayer, was completed in 1263.

3. *'Our Father' in the* Catena Aurea (*St Luke*)

Pope Urban died in 1264. The glosses on the other three Gospels were not completed until 1267. They were dedicated to Thomas's friend and former pupil, Cardinal Annibaldo degli Annibaldi. When Thomas arrived at ch. 11, vv. 1 to 4, of St Luke's Gospel (the section which contains the text of the Lord's Prayer) he was able, once again, to draw together an impressive number of texts from the Fathers of the Church. The *Catena Aurea* itself, taken as a whole, might well appear as an arbitrary collection of disparate citations. That, however, is by no means the measure of its achievement, nor is it a summary of what it represents. For, carefully read, the *Catena* reveals to us something of Thomas's own interpretive genius, and indeed something also of his own theological vision. 'Other compilations exhibit research, industry, learning; but this, though a mere compilation, evinces a masterly command over the whole subject of theology.'[2]

4. *'Our Father' in* The Lectures on St Matthew

St Thomas delivered a series of lectures on the Gospel of St Matthew during his second regency at Paris, probably between

[1] For a helpful introduction to the *Catena Aurea*, see Aidan Nichols, O.P., 'Introduction to the 1997 Edition', *Catena Aurea*, Vol 1, St Matthew, ed. John Henry Newman (London: 1999; first published 1841) pp. v–xvii.
[2] M. Pattison (ed.), *Commentary on the Four Gospels by St Thomas Aquinas*, Vol 1 (Oxford: 1864) pp. iii–iv.

the years 1270–71.[3] The lectures have come down to us in the form of two *reportationes*, one by a Dominican called Peter of Andria and another, a less full report, by a Parisian cleric called Léger of Besançon. When, in his lectures, Thomas arrived at ch. 6 of St Matthew's Gospel, vv. 9 to 15 (the section which contains the text of the Lord's Prayer) he took care to give every single word in the prayer particular attention, and the observations he made were both practical and profound. Not surprisingly, therefore, this section in the commentary represents one of the undoubted highlights of the entire work.

5. *'Our Father' in the* Summa theologiae

The longest Question in the *Summa theologiae* (Question 83 in *Secunda Secundae*) is concerned exclusively with prayer, a fact which indicates the enormous importance Thomas attaches to the subject. The actual date when Thomas composed Question 83 is uncertain, but May–June 1271 has been suggested as one possibility.[4] Article 9 in Question 83 has, as its sole object of interest, the Lord's Prayer.

6. *'Our Father' in the Sermon-Conferences at Naples*

During the Lent of 1273, at Naples, St Thomas preached a series of sermons on the Our Father. 'So great', we are told, 'was his reputation for sanctity' that he attracted huge crowds.[5] The sermons were delivered in the vernacular, the language of

---

[3] See Tugwell, *Albert and Thomas: Selected Writings*, pp. 246–7, and p. 332, note 464.
[4] See *Albert and Thomas*, pp. 272–3.
[5] The witness who heard Thomas preaching on the Lord's Prayer, on this occasion, was a certain Jean Coppa. See *Fontes, Processus* LXXXVII, p. 291.

the local people. Taken down, initially, in the form of notes, they were later edited by Thomas's faithful assistant, Brother Reginald, and then translated into Latin.[6] It has been suggested that the original notes may have been touched up by Reginald to make them sound more acceptably academic and scholastic. Fortunately, however, enough of the original form and flavour of the sermons has survived to help explain why the faithful, in that Lent of 1273, turned out in such huge numbers to hear St Thomas preach.[7]

7. *'Our Father' in the* Compendium of Theology

Scholars have long debated exactly when Aquinas composed this remarkable text. Some were convinced that it belonged to an early period in Thomas's academic career; others were of the opinion that it was dictated in the very last years of Thomas's life at Naples. It now appears that both views were, in some measure, correct. The first part of the book, dealing with the virtue of faith, was probably composed when Thomas was at Rome (1265–67); the second part, dealing with the virtue of hope, probably composed at Naples (1272–73).[8] There is a special quality in the tone and atmosphere of this second part of the *Compendium.* The entire focus of Thomas's attention is on the Our Father, a prayer which he sees as manifesting in a particular way the virtue of hope. Here, even more than usual,

[6]   See Tugwell, *Albert and Thomas*, p. 338, note 554.
[7]   For further information about Thomas as preacher, see Jean-Pierre Torrell, 'La pratique pastorale d'un théologien du XIII siecle: Thomas d'Aquin predicateur', *Recherches thomasiennes: études revues et augmentées* (Paris: 2000) pp. 282–312. For a recent edition of other sermons by St Thomas, see *Saint Thomas d'Aquin: Sermons*, ed. J. Ménard (Paris: Éditions du Sandre, 2004).
[8]   This is the conclusion reached by H.-F. Dondaine, the principal editor of the Leonine edition of the text. See *Compendium theologiae*, p. 8.

Thomas appears in serene command of his material. But the work, unfortunately, was never completed, being interrupted we may presume (as the *Summa theologiae* was interrupted) by the decision of St Thomas, after an intense mystical experience, not to continue with his theological writing. This event occurred on the 6 December 1273.[9]

---

[9] At this time St Thomas also suffered an almost complete physical collapse. See James A. Weisheipl, *Friar Thomas d'Aquin: His Life, Thought and Works*, pp. 320–3.

Index

1401812R0

Printed in Great Britain by
Amazon.co.uk, Ltd.,
Marston Gate.